Praises For

Walking with the Beatitudes

Like many concepts tossed around in Christian circles, the Beatitudes are often referenced but not always deeply understood. A centerpoint of Jesus' teaching and the launchpad for his larger Sermon on the Mount, they deserve more careful study and intentional application than often given. Utilizing Biblical study, keen insight, practical examples, and personal vulnerability, Amy Blindt leads the reader on a meaningful journey toward deeper understanding and embodiment of "the blessed life" as Jesus defines it. My own faith was enriched and challenged, and I recommend it to any who seek to faithfully follow Jesus.

—**Rev. Stacy Cochran Nowell**, Senior Pastor, *First Baptist Church Huntersville*

***

I found Amy's book to be challenging and comforting at the same time. Challenging in that I'm reminded just how far I have to go in my journey to become like Jesus; comforting in that Amy provides sound insight and practical steps for making progress in that endeavor! Thanks Amy for shedding helpful light and providing powerful depth to these simple, yet penetratingly profound statements from the lips of Jesus!

—**Andre Riendeau,** Lead Pastor, *Wintonbury Church, Bloomfield, CT*

Walking with the Beatitudes

Bible Study by Amy M. Blindt

Published by KHARIS PUBLISHING, an imprint of KHARIS MEDIA LLC.

Copyright © 2021 Amy M. Blindt

ISBN-13: 978-1-63746-102-0

ISBN-10: 1-63746-102-X

Library of Congress Control Number: 2021950407

All rights reserved. This book or parts thereof may not be reproduced in any form, stored in a retrieval system, or transmitted in any form by any means - electronic, mechanical, photocopy, recording, or otherwise - without prior written permission of the publisher, except as provided by United States of America copyright law.

Unless otherwise noted, scripture is taken from THE HOLY BIBLE, NEW INTERNATIONAL VERSION ®. Copyright© 1973, 1978, 1984, 2011 by Biblica, Inc.™. Used by permission of Zondervan

All KHARIS PUBLISHING products are available at special quantity discounts for bulk purchase for sales promotions, premiums, fund-raising, and educational needs. For details, contact:

Kharis Media LLC
Tel: 1-479-599-8657
support@kharispublishing.com
www.kharispublishing.com

CONTENTS

Preface vii

Sections 1 – 2: Introduction
1. Choosing the Beatitudes 1
2. Identity and Wisdom in the Beatitudes 4

Sections 3 – 8: Poor in Spirit
3. Definition 8
4. Biblical Example 10
5. Stumbling Blocks 13
6. Modern Example 16
7. Challenge 20
8. Conclusion 24

Sections 9 – 14: Mourn
9. Definition 28
10. Biblical Example 30
11. Stumbling Blocks 33
12. Modern Example 35
13. Challenge 39
14. Conclusion 41

Sections 15 – 20: Meek
15. Definition 45
16. Biblical Example 48
17. Stumbling Blocks 51
18. Modern Example 54
19. Challenge 57
20. Conclusion 59

Sections 21 – 26: Hunger & Thirst for Righteousness
21. Definition 63
22. Biblical Example 66
23. Stumbling Blocks 69
24. Modern Example 72
25. Challenge 75
26. Conclusion 77

Sections 27 – 32: Merciful
27. Definition 81
28. Biblical Example 83
29. Stumbling Blocks 86
30. Modern Example 89

31	Challenge...	92
32	Conclusion..	94

Sections 33 – 38: Pure in Heart

33	Definition...	97
34	Biblical Example...	99
35	Stumbling Blocks...	102
36	Modern Example..	104
37	Challenge..	107
38	Conclusion..	109

Sections 39 – 44: Peacemakers

39	Definition..	112
40	Biblical Example...	114
41	Stumbling Blocks..	117
42	Modern Example..	119
43	Challenge..	122
44	Conclusion...	125

Sections 45 – 50: Persecuted Because of Righteousness

45	Definition...	128
46	Biblical Example...	130
47	Stumbling Blocks...	133
48	Modern Example..	135
49	Challenge..	137
50	Conclusion...	139

Sections 51 – 52: Conclusion

51	Full Circle..	142
52	Walking with the Beatitudes......................................	144

Preface

This is a deep dive study of Matthew 5:3-10. In the scripture, Jesus teaches eight principles, known as Beatitudes. This book is designed to be read once a week for an entire year or as a daily devotional for 7 or 8 weeks. We will spend six sections meditating on each Beatitude, with 2 Introduction and 2 Conclusion sections.

> Sections/Weeks 1-2: Introduction
> Sections/Weeks 3-8: Poor in Spirit
> Sections/Weeks 9-14: Mourn
> Sections/Weeks 15-20: Meek
> Sections/Weeks21-26: Hunger and Thirst for Righteousness
> Sections/Weeks 27-32: Merciful
> Sections/Weeks 33-38: Pure in Heart
> Sections/Weeks 39-44: Peacemakers
> Sections/Weeks 45-50: Persecuted Because of Righteousness
> Sections/Weeks 51-52: Conclusion

The six sections spent on each Beatitude will be broken out into this schedule:

Section 1: Definition. Exploring the technical meanings of the words used in the verse.
Section 2: Biblical Example. Looking at a character or story in the Bible where this Beatitude is relevant.
Section 3: Stumbling Blocks. Discussing some of the biggest hindrances preventing us from walking in this Beatitude.
Section 4: Modern Example. Looking at a more recent example of someone who exhibited this Beatitude and what we can learn from them.
Section 5: Challenge. Applying what we've learned so far about this Beatitude and how it can be relevant to our lives.
Section 6: Conclusion. Summarizing the Beatitude and looking at the blessing Jesus has attached to it.

Sections 1 – 2

Introduction

1

Introduction: Choosing the Beatitudes

One summer, my son was memorizing the Beatitudes as part of a school assignment. Every day I would overhear him practicing in an almost rhythmic recitation—learning the sounds of the words together--rather than the words themselves. At age 8, the concepts and even some of the terms are foreign and difficult to understand. Even as an adult, I find some of the ideas and words difficult to understand on a practical level. However, memorizing and reciting this powerful passage of the scripture is like a seed that has been planted in his heart.

The seed may lie dormant for years until it is watered and can begin to grow, but it remains there in his subconscious and spirit. Similarly, I believe that the Beatitudes are a seed in my own heart. The words have been read or heard periodically throughout my life; however, their true significance lays dormant and full of potential.

Daily hearing my son's robotic recitation of the Beatitudes began to water the seed that lay dormant in my heart. I found the verses of Matthew 5 frequently coming to mind. Finally, one afternoon I was driving to a lunch date with my husband and mulling over, "Blessed are those who hunger and thirst after righteousness, for they shall be filled." *How do I get to that point where I seek righteousness before food?* I wondered to myself. I want it, but I am a fleshly being, so I instinctively hunger and thirst for food and drink. Yet I want to be blessed, and I want to be filled!

By the time I arrived at my destination, the entire concept of this study was kind of downloaded into my brain from Above. I had to wait for Steve, so I made notes on my phone and outlined the entire thing. I knew that I wanted to have my heart transformed by the Beatitudes, and I wanted to share this experience with others.

The many steps of obedience that I am called to take are those that did not make my "To Do" list for the day! They come about from having a heart that is listening for the Lord's whisper or allowing myself to be guided by the Holy Spirit. I was not planning for this study, and I certainly don't have all the answers to my questions. I feel unprepared to facilitate this discussion, but I am confident that God will use me in my inadequacies.

I believe that each of the characteristics described by the Beatitudes allows us to be even more in tune with the Holy Spirit and God's will. Subsequently, I believe that these characteristics will help us gain wisdom because of how our hearts will be shaped.

The Beatitudes are not a set of commands, just as the pursuit of godly wisdom is not a command. Instead, these verses are a series of teaching statements. If Jesus chose to have these be the introduction to His longest recorded Sermon, then there must be more significant value to them than just something to memorize and recite. Jesus is teaching us something significant—let's pray for the wisdom to understand!

> *Matthew 5:3-10*
> *Blessed are the poor in spirit,*
> *for theirs is the Kingdom of Heaven.*
> *Blessed are those who mourn,*
> *for they will be comforted.*
> *Blessed are the meek,*
> *for they will inherit the Earth.*
> *Blessed are those who hunger and thirst for righteousness,*
> *for they will be filled.*
> *Blessed are the merciful,*
> *for they will be shown mercy.*
> *Blessed are the pure in heart,*
> *for they will see God.*
> *Blessed are the peacemakers,*
> *for they will be called children of God.*
> *Blessed are those who are persecuted because of righteousness,*
> *for theirs is the Kingdom of Heaven.*

To think and pray about:

1. As you read through the Beatitudes, do any jump out as the ones you particularly want to understand or focus on?

2. These verses all begin with "blessed." Blessing can be a vague concept—not a concrete calculation of positive life experiences or a

list of Amazon packages we will receive on our doorstep from God. I've read somewhere that the word, 'blessing' means inheritance. What are your expectations when you anticipate blessings from God? Have you been disappointed in the past when your expectations of blessings do not match their reality?

3. As mentioned, the Beatitudes are not commands but teachings. What is your motivation to understand and follow Jesus' teachings?

As you pray this week, ask God for a teachable heart. Ask Him to help you listen to the roots of what He would have you learn—not just what appears on the surface. Thank Him for the teachings of Jesus, which both shape our hearts and show us God's heart.

Dear Lord, thank you for this study. Thank you that we can journey together even though we are apart physically. Thank you for the Beatitudes and the wisdom contained in them. Please give us unified insight into how we can apply this scripture to our lives. Lord, thank you for being a faithful God who listens to our prayers. Help us to be continually reminded of you this week—your words coming to us at the right times so that we can respond to every situation with the grace and strength we have in you. In Jesus' Name, Amen!

2

Introduction: Identity and Wisdom in the Beatitudes

Part 1: Identity

My name is Amy, and I love coffee. That's a pretty accurate statement since I drink coffee daily. It is part of my routine, I enjoy it, and it is comforting to me.

But what if I said, "My name is Amy, and I am a coffee lover"? Or someone introduced me as "Amy, the coffee lover"? It sounds like a more intense relationship between myself and coffee, right? Instead of just being a person who enjoys coffee, I am now defined and characterized by this love of coffee.

In the first introduction, the verb is "love," which is an action verb. I choose to act in a way that shows I love coffee. In the second introduction, the verb is "am," which is a state of being. It's an identity. I am identifying myself as a coffee lover. It is who I am. The third introduction uses "the," which is also a way to show identity. It is how others perceive me.

In history, Alexander the Great is remembered as being "Great"! He is not Alexander, who also had some greatness. Being "the Great" is his historical identity, and it distinguishes him from every other Alexander I've ever heard of. To be called "the something" is a big deal, but not always good. If my identity was Amy the Lazy, that's not very flattering.

It occurs to me that the way Jesus taught the Beatitudes was significant because he used "the" to describe these blessed people. He didn't say, "Blessed are the people who have meekness," He said, "Blessed are THE meek." The people identified by their meekness are those that are blessed, not people who just exhibit the characteristic occasionally.

As we go through this study, keep in mind that we want our hearts to be transformed at a deeper level, other than just understanding. We want to learn to exhibit these characteristics to the point where they are a noticeable part of our Christian walk.

Part 2: Wisdom

In the previous chapter, I mentioned that I believe the Beatitudes are not only a description of blessing but also a source of wisdom. The characteristics (poor in spirit, those who mourn, meek, hunger and thirst for righteousness, merciful, pure in heart, peacemakers, and persecuted) are mentioned elsewhere throughout scripture so that we can glean wisdom simply through study. However, the most striking occurrence of this is found in James 3.

> *"Who is wise and understanding among you? Let them show it by their good life, by deeds done in the humility that comes from wisdom. But if you harbor bitter envy and selfish ambition in your hearts, do not boast about it or deny the truth. Such "wisdom" does not come down from heaven but is earthly, unspiritual, demonic. For where you have envy and selfish ambition, there you find disorder and every evil practice.*
>
> *But the wisdom that comes from heaven is first of all pure; then peace-loving, considerate, submissive, full of mercy and good fruit, impartial and sincere. Peacemakers who sow in peace reap a harvest of righteousness."* **James 3:13-18**

Verses 17 and 18 are especially significant because if you look at the list of things that wisdom is and compare it to the list of Beatitudes, there is a lot of overlap! Some words are not exact but rather synonymous (like meek and submissive). But I find it very interesting how the characteristics of wisdom are also the characteristics of those who are blessed.

For example, wisdom is full of mercy, and "blessed are the merciful." We can therefore conclude that becoming merciful is also a means to becoming wise. If you are seeking wisdom, then be merciful.

Another interesting example is that James says wisdom loves peace and that if you are sowing peace, you will reap righteousness. That's great for someone who is hungering and thirsting for righteousness! If they want to find that righteousness, then they should seek peace-loving wisdom!

And what about the pure in heart? James says that the wisdom that comes from heaven is first of all pure! Jesus says that the pure in heart will see God, who is obviously the source of heavenly wisdom. So if we are pure in heart, not only are we blessed—per Jesus' teachings—we are also able to see wisdom.

To think and pray about:

1. What parts of your character would people choose to label you with? How would you label yourself? Do they match because you present an honest version of yourself, or have you created a false public identity for the sake of pleasing people?

2. Would you prefer to be described differently? What "the" do you want to be known as?

3. Is there anything in the James 3 passage that particularly stands out to you in this season of life?

As you pray this week, ask God for wisdom in your identity. Allow Him to show you who you are as His creation, and be humble to accept correction where it is needed. Pray for guidance in seeking heavenly wisdom in all things.

Dear Lord, thank you for this study. Thank you that we can explore your Word together and meditate on it. Please open our spiritual eyes to see how we can apply these scriptures to our lives. Please help us remain focused on you and not ourselves as we seek to honor and glorify you with our obedience. In Jesus' Name, Amen!

Sections 3 – 8

Poor in Spirit

3

Poor in Spirit: Definition

"Blessed are the poor in spirit, for theirs is the kingdom of heaven." **Matthew 5:3**

When skimming over the Beatitudes list, it seems like Jesus repeated himself with the beatitudes of Poor in Spirit and Meek. I frequently hear the word humble applied to both, which seems appropriate and could make them synonymous. However, if we look at the Greek words used, we see a stark difference in meanings. The Greek word used for "poor" in Poor in Spirit is *"ptochos,"* which means "to crouch or cower as one helpless." For Meek, the word used is *"praus,"* which means "strength under authority" or "power under control." So there is quite a bit of difference between the meanings of the two Beatitudes!

Poor in Spirit implies poverty. And poverty means having nothing. It implies insignificance. It implies complete dependence on the benevolence of someone else. To be Poor in Spirit is to recognize that without God, we are nothing and have nothing. "Poor in Spirit" is the humility that comes from acknowledging our dependence and helplessness.

Do you think there is some significance in Jesus beginning His list with Poor in Spirit? I do! This realization that we are reliant upon God is critical in preparing our hearts for the other Beatitudes. Recognizing our depravity sets us up for gratitude for what God has done for us in kindness, and this kindness leads us to repent. Without repentance, why would we even want to bother with anything else of God?

"Or do you show contempt for the riches of his kindness, forbearance, and patience, not realizing that God's kindness is intended to lead you to repentance?" **Romans 2:4**

If we are rich, do we really need the kindness of others to get by? Without being Poor in Spirit, I think it is easy even for Christians to fall into an attitude of pseudo-self-sufficiency. We can fool ourselves into thinking we can earn our salvation through our efforts and talents. We can forget that all we have is due to the grace of God, and therefore we do not recognize our spiritual poverty. We can think we have all the answers and therefore stop asking God for directions.

But how do we know we need God? How do we recognize our complete dependency on Him?

> *"Through him, all things were made; without him, nothing was made that has been made." ***John 1:3***

If He made everything, and we can make nothing, it sounds like everything belongs to God; all of the Earth and air, justice and mercy, the tangible and intangible. That leaves us with nothing that He has not given us. We are poor and indebted to Him. Additionally...

> *"For all have sinned and fall short of the glory of God." ***Romans 3:23***

That means all the glory is His, too, as is any redemptive power. We cannot make anything ourselves, and we cannot save ourselves. We are poor and indebted to Him.

We have nothing and can be nothing without God. When we recognize this and live with a posture of humility that this brings, we are Poor in Spirit.

To think and pray about:

1. What reminds you of the greatness of God and your personal insignificance?
2. Do you think your sin helps you to remember that you are nothing without God? Or does it get in your way?
3. If poverty of spirit is a blessed identity to have, why do you think it seems so unattractive?

Dear Lord, thank you for this week. Thank you for showing us that spiritual poverty leads to spiritual blessing. Please help us to understand this better as we seek to give up control to you. Let us be stewards of what you have given us, not owners, so that we may recognize our dependence on you. Let us be humbly aware of our shortcomings but also peacefully grateful that you love us anyway. In Jesus' Name, Amen!

4

Poor in Spirit: Biblical Example

"Blessed are the poor in spirit, for theirs is the kingdom of heaven." **Matthew 5:3**

For a Biblical example of Poor in Spirit, let's take a look at Gideon. Gideon was born during a time of fear. The Israelites were living under the oppression of the Midianites, and "Midian so impoverished the Israelites that they cried out to the Lord for help." (Judges 6:6)

When the Angel of The Lord came to Gideon, he was threshing wheat in a winepress because he was afraid the Midianites would come to steal it. The Angel of The Lord gave Gideon the assignment to save Israel from Midian, but Gideon questioned this by telling the Angel: "My clan is the weakest in Manasseh, and I am the least in my family."

Gideon wholly owns up to his poverty, his weakness, and his status. Without the benevolence of God, Gideon was literally a cowardly nobody. He was Poor in Spirit, although he had not yet learned to depend on God to balance out this poverty. So, because he was also poor in faith, he did not immediately act on God's calling.

God is gracious, and so He helped strengthen Gideon's faith through a series of signs—each one requiring more faith from Gideon to accomplish. Like exercising spiritual muscles, God called Gideon to do more incrementally complicated tasks. We read that Gideon was afraid but obedient. His obedience began this cycle: obedience leading to deeper faith, to more complex tasks of obedience, leading to deeper faith, etc.

We don't read very much about Gideon's attitude during the process that eventually defeats the Midianites. However, because we know Gideon's history and the logic-defying instructions God gave him we also know that Gideon cannot take any personal credit for the victory. He was utterly dependent on God, and everyone knew it. Also, because of his poverty of spirit, he does not argue with God. Once his faith is strengthened, Gideon completes the tasks without question.

God could have only used someone who was Poor in Spirit for this story of victory. Had He used someone who already had earthly influence, then that person may have gotten credit for rallying the men. Had He used someone with military experience, then that person may have argued against the strange plan God had. Had He used someone with a lot of self-confidence, then that person may have tried to fight in their own strength. But each step of God's plan required complete dependence upon Him. Gideon deeply needed God, and he deeply knew it!

Now, just as we all have seasons of life where we are spiritually strong and seasons where we are spiritually weak, Gideon did not remain poor in Spirit. In the middle of Chapter 8, things shifted for Gideon. The victory has been won, and the Israelites approached Gideon to be their king. He refuses the position, but he does ask for a share of the plunder from each man. From there, "Gideon made the gold into an ephod, which he placed in Ophrah, his town. All Israel prostituted themselves by worshipping it there, and it became a snare to Gideon and his family." (Judges 8:27)

What went wrong? He was a great man of faith, humbly Poor in Spirit, and then… he wasn't… "Interestingly, I don't think that taking the plunder was the stumbling block for Gideon—it's what he did with it. Had he bought some land for his family to live on, perhaps donated it to the poor, or maybe sent his sons to be educated, I think the outcome would have been different. The problem was that he created a literal idol from the gold. And not only did he make an idol, he gave himself and his town a reputation of importance by allowing it to be worshipped publicly. Gideon did not feel a strong dependence on God anymore—he was admired and important, he was financially secure, and his enemies had been defeated. Instead of worshipping the God who provided all of this, he and Israel worshipped the provision itself.

The ephod was the symbol of the miraculous deliverance and provision God had orchestrated. It became a snare because Gideon no longer had the deep knowledge that he was dependent upon God. He was no longer Poor in Spirit but relatively Rich in Flesh. Gideon was very blessed. He went on to have 70 sons and was able to provide for them. He lived to a good age, and there was peace in the land for the rest of his life. He had the Lord's favor, which is great, but the future of his legacy and family was marred because they no longer sought the Lord.

To be Poor in Spirit is to depend on God more than we depend on anything else. It is to acknowledge deep within our hearts that anything we have is from Him, and He must therefore be the object of our worship. The literal poor have an advantage in this because they do not have as much that could become a snare. Those of us who have been blessed with much need to learn how to keep all that we have held out to God, wholly dependent on Him to give and take away. Even our talents and gifts can become snares if we begin to rely on them instead of the God who gave them to us!

To think and pray about:

1. Read Judges 6-8. Does anything else about this story stand out to you?

2. Do you find it easier to be obedient when you have nothing and are desperate, like Gideon? Or are you more willing to obey when you have a safety net of sorts?

3. Can you think of any other Bible stories or verses about being Poor in Spirit? What lessons can we learn from them?

Dear Lord, thank you for this day which you have given us. Thank you for being our provider, our Savior, and our healer. Please help us remember to hold everything we have out to you so that it does not become a snare in our lives. Help us to keep our eyes fixed on you so that we have the courage to ignore everything else around us and be obedient. Thank you for your patience and mercy as we seek to learn these lessons at a deeper level. In Jesus' Name, Amen!

5

Poor in Spirit: Stumbling Blocks

"Blessed are the poor in spirit, for theirs is the kingdom of heaven." **Matthew 5:3**

What makes a poor person not be poor anymore? Ownership! It may seem silly or obvious when simply put, but it's the truth! Someone is no longer considered poor when they start owning stuff. It's all relative, of course. A middle-class American's concept of poor will be different than someone in a 3rd world country's concept. But when you own what you need, you are no longer poor in that category. You are no longer dependent on an outside party to provide it for you—you already own it!

There is security with ownership. Control. Self-sufficiency. Pride. I like all of those feelings! But having them means I am no longer poor. If my goal is to be Poor in Spirit, then I must remember that there is much more to give away than just ownership of physical possessions. Relying on my own strength, wisdom, hope, courage, etc., also prevents me from being Poor in Spirit. If I am personally rich in those areas, I will have a much more difficult time depending on God in them.

It's such a conundrum! If we have stuff, which means we can't be Poor in Spirit, should we just become pitiful bums, living on the street and daily praying that God will send us a piece of bread? But then not having anything means nothing gets done. If we have no strength, how can we serve others? If we have no wisdom, how can we make Godly decisions? If we have no hope, how will we even worship the God who created us? And if we do not have what we need for our physical bodies, how will we honor them as temples of God? Being Poor in Spirit seems to negate all of the Bible verses about being richly blessed and getting what we need from God. If He is giving us stuff—how can we be poor? And then why would Jesus say that being Poor in Spirit leads to blessing?

But I don't think that He intends for us to be bums at all. God loves us and wants to provide for our needs. He wants us to receive strength, hope, faith, joy, etc. So I think the major key here is STEWARDSHIP, not OWNERSHIP. Stewardship implies possessing without owning. A steward takes care of what he has been given, but when he leaves that position, the things remain with the owner.

Being Poor in Spirit means enjoying the many blessings that God gives us, but with the attitude and realization that they are His to own and ours to manage. When our spirit is poor, we depend on God even when we know that our next meal is already in our refrigerator. We rely on Him for wisdom even when we are smart enough to solve a problem. Our spirit knows that He has given us these things to use—but they belong to Him.

How do we adopt this mindset? I think it's easier to wrap our minds around the importance of surrendering the tangible things and giving them to God. But as I was praying about the intangibles like strength, joy, etc., I began to realize that even these must be given up if we are truly going to be Poor in Spirit. If we ask God to give us strength, then it becomes ours. But if we ask God to BE our strength, then the strength remains with Him—the Source.

Imagine you are going to iron some clothes (or ironing bead projects which are more likely to be found in my house! ☺). You plug in the iron and let it heat up. And then you bend down to the electrical outlet, tell it "thank you" for the heat, unplug it, and begin to iron. Why would you do that? You'll be able to accomplish some of your ironing because of the heat provided, but the iron will start to cool off once it is disconnected from the heat source. How silly!

And yet, spiritually, when we try to own what God is giving us, it loses power too. We can pray, "God give me joy!," He provides us with some joy, we take it with a "thank you!", and then we walk away going about our business. But how much more powerful it is if our provision remains connected to the Source! We can pray, "God, BE my joy." Lord, don't give me strength, BE my strength; don't save me, BE my salvation. Don't give me hope, BE my hope; don't send me provision, BE my provider.

See the difference? All of these blessings are ours to use while they remain in their Source. We don't need to own them—we can be poor and still have everything we need because we are connected to that Source of everything we need. We can be Poor in Spirit when our spirit forgoes ownership and instead settles for stewardship.

For the record, I do not believe that asking God to give us strength, joy, hope, etc., is in any way wrong or sinful. I just know that words are powerful, and the way we phrase things can also be powerful. So communicating a request in a way that reminds us to stay connected to the Source might be just what we need to remember actually to do it! ☺

Being Poor in Spirit might not be so bad after all!

To think and pray about:

1. Becoming Poor in Spirit is difficult for me because it means giving up control and self-sufficiency. Are those the stumbling blocks you face too, or do you have other stumbling blocks keeping you from becoming Poor in Spirit?

2. What do you need most from God right now? Ask Him to "be" that thing instead of just giving it to you, and see if your perspective changes.

3. Read John 15:1-17. Like the iron when plugged in, we can accomplish much more spiritually when connected to the Source. If we would remain in Jesus, as He tells us to, do you think it would also be easier to be Poor in Spirit?

Dear Lord, thank you for the wisdom you've given to us in the Bible. Thank you for being our salvation and our hope. Thank you for being our strength and our peace. Thank you for being our provider and our rock. Thank you for the reminder that everything we have is yours. Help us to honor you with what you've allowed us to be stewards of; our time, energy, talents, money, possessions, etc. Let us be in the habit of continually surrendering ownership of them so that we may be Poor in Spirit despite being richly blessed. In Jesus' Name, Amen!

6

Poor in Spirit: Modern Example

"Blessed are the poor in spirit, for theirs is the kingdom of heaven."
Matthew 5:3

George Muller was a modern man who was Poor in Spirit. I use the term "modern" loosely because he's been dead over a hundred years already! However, I think that his life and legacy hold much value for study. The way he approached decision-making and finances showed his dependence on God, which allowed him to significantly impact the world for God's glory.

George was born into a wealthy family and given much freedom by his father. George enjoyed having money and eventually began stealing through various cons. Even while he was in seminary, he stole and did not take his studies seriously. He was not exactly an obvious candidate to become a great man of faith!

One day, a friend invited George to a prayer meeting. Although he was in seminary, George preferred to go to parties and bars and places to gamble. However, something stirred within George at the invitation, and he accepted. This invitation led to George discovering true faith versus the theology in his books. He began training to become a missionary instead of just a comfortably paid pastor. George became determined to rely solely on God to supply his needs.

He married a woman who was willing to walk with him on this faith journey. Together, they leaned on God to supply what was needed, and the Lord always proved Himself faithful. It wasn't always easy, however, as this excerpt from a biography explains:

> *"The next year, 1831, would be one of intense trial. Many times there was not a single shilling in the Muller home. Then, at the right time, as the Mullers continued looking to God, their reward would arrive in the form of money and supplies.*
>
> *God allowed the Mullers' faith to be strenuously tried on January 6,7, and 8. All their money was gone. George prayed earnestly and faithfully, but still, nothing came. The Mullers were tempted to distrust the Lord. Then George remembered God's faithfulness up to this time: "He had not only supplied all our needs but had given us many miraculous answers to prayer. I began to think it would be of no use to trust in the Lord this time. Perhaps I had gone too far in living by faith. But praise the Lord! This trial lasted only a few minutes. He enabled me to trust in Him, and Satan was immediately defeated!"*
>
> *Some ten minutes later, when George returned to his room, the Lord sent deliverance. "A sister brought us two pounds, four shillings. The Lord triumphed, and our faith was strengthened.""*

What a testimony! George and his wife knew they needed God. The way they lived their lives proved it. They went on to open orphanages and schools in England—relying solely on God to provide for their needs. George Muller's ministry impacted over 10,000 orphans, and the testimony of his life has inspired countless other people. He intentionally did not ask people for money but instead relied on God to divinely inspire people to give. His conviction was to spend his energy serving people, not fundraising.

But what might have happened if, during that trial period of their faith on January 6-8, 1831, the Mullers had decided to work things out for themselves? After three days of no provision, what if George had become fearful and sought provision apart from God? His faith would not have been strengthened through the trial. In fact, it may have led him to lead a life of limited faith and limited impact. Fortunately (for many), George was able to continue to trust God despite his initial uneasiness. It was just one trial out of many that led to deeper and deeper faith.

There are so many things to learn from the life of George Muller. I am reminded of Luke 16:10, which says, "whoever can be trusted with very little can also be trusted with much." While this verse is speaking about God trusting *us*, the principle of trust goes both ways. George remembered, amid his trial, that God had always been faithful before—so He should be trusted again. Each time George depended on God and then waited for God to prove His faithfulness, George's faith was strengthened.

Can we not do the same? In those trials, where we feel vulnerable and exposed because we have given up control (or never had it, to begin with), we can look back on God's previous faithfulness to us to draw courage. One of the best ways to defeat the Enemy is to stop listening to him and start praising God for all the good things He has done!

George chose to be Poor in Spirit. He willingly gave up his inheritance from his father and the pursuit of a well-paying career. George could have been a respectable pastor with a stable income, which would have probably blessed his congregation just fine. He had a natural aptitude and would have been successful in his own way. However, George chose God's best instead of his own because he adopted the attitude of being Poor in Spirit. George loved God and recognized that truly honoring and serving Him required the complete surrender of his personal agenda. He became an available vessel for God to use, and subsequently, his legacy still glorifies God.

In contrast, Gideon did not choose to be Poor in Spirit—he and the Israelites were pretty much at rock bottom. It's easier to trust God with big things when our choices are limited. Gideon still did have a choice, however, and he chose faith. But just think of it, the reason that the Israelites needed rescuing was that they "did evil in the eyes of the Lord" (Judges 6:1). That is literally how the story of Gideon begins. The Israelites were brought into poverty because they were not obeying God. It was through rebuke and discipline that Gideon knew he must depend on God.

God used both of these men who were Poor in Spirit, despite the differences in how they got there. It is an excellent testament to how He redeems all things! But I think it's worth noting that there are areas in my life where maybe I should be George and other areas where I'm Gideon. When I am Poor in Spirit out of desperation, God will use it if I am willing to let Him lead. However, how much greater is it if things are going tolerably well and I surrender them anyway! Perhaps, my own abilities seem good enough, my bank account is comfortable, my health is good, my roof has no leaks, my hope is secure, etc. I should be like George and give control of them to God before I am desperate. God will honor this faithful surrender of control and be able to use my willing availability to glorify Himself.

Gideon's surrender was triggered by fear. George's surrender was inspired by love and appreciation for the Lord. Both men, however, had their faith strengthened by remembering God's past faithfulness. The Enemy does not want our faith to be strengthened. He will try to discourage us and get us to do things in our own strength and timing. "Submit yourselves, then, to God. Resist the devil, and he will flee from you. Come near to God, and He will come near to you." (James 4:7-8a). God wants us to depend on Him. He wants us to become Poor in Spirit because He loves us. If we are Poor in Spirit, we will remain in Him and therefore be richly blessed.

To think and pray about this week:

1. Can you think of any other modern examples of people who are overwhelmingly Poor in Spirit? Perhaps someone you know, or maybe a well-known hero of the faith? What other lessons can you learn from them to apply to your journey?

2. Do you have any areas of your life where you feel like Gideon? Perhaps to surrender seems more accessible as you think there is no other option? Although it is not necessarily comfortable, thank God for the opportunity He has given you to become Poor in Spirit. If you are willing to proceed with patient faith, God will indeed honor your yielding to Him and bring you into a story that glorifies Him and blesses you.

3. Do you have any areas of your life where you should be George? Perhaps you have a choice on whether to proceed by faith or by your strength. Ask God to help you identify some of those areas that you haven't even thought to surrender! Ask Him for courage in letting them go so that you become a steward instead of an owner.

Dear Lord, thank you for this day. Thank you for George Muller and the powerful example he set. Thank you for giving us the opportunity to surrender control of even the "successful" areas of our lives. Thank you for being a faithful God whose faithfulness defeats the lies of the Enemy. Let the past stories of your grace and goodness get us through the challenges we face in our faith. Let us become more and more dependent on you as we become willing and available vessels to your Word. In Jesus' Name, Amen!

7

Poor in Spirit: Challenge

"Blessed are the poor in spirit, for theirs is the kingdom of heaven."
Matthew 5:3

I had a very restless night recently. I felt anxious about the uncertainty of the future, and I felt very inadequate to do the things I have been called to do. Who am I to be a leader? Why should I offer anyone any advice or insight? How dare I try to write a book? I am no one!

I felt very Poor in Spirit, possibly how Gideon must have felt while threshing wheat in a winepress. Why should God use me? I am afraid. The vulnerability of this poverty is not pleasant. I don't want to give up the small amount of control I think I have.

However, the longer I cling to the pseudo-comfort of control, the longer that fear will last. I think being on the verge of surrender is probably the scariest. But that's precisely where being Poor in Spirit leads: the edge of submission. Once there, Poor in Spirit, I have a choice. I have already acknowledged that I need God because I am Poor in Spirit, but that doesn't mean I automatically trust Him with my needs. An intentional step of faith is required.

Imagine being in the lobby of a very tall building. You want to get to the top floor—hundreds of floors up. There are stairs or an elevator—the choice is yours! But you are sensible, so you know that you'll never be able to walk up all of those stairs. You fully acknowledge that the elevator is the only way to get you to where you need to be. However, you walk over to it and just stand there. You aren't sure that you trust this device—it's intimidating. To get onto the elevator is to give up control and surrender yourself to its mechanisms. You won't be able to control the speed at which you go up, you won't be able to prevent any stops along the way, and you won't be able to manage even your own safety! If the elevator fails—you are going down with it! You look back at the stairs, appreciating the control you have on them. It's tempting to try them even though you know you would not get to where you are supposed to be.

Getting on an elevator requires faith in that elevator. You can be totally convinced that you cannot get up to the top of the building without the elevator, but until you take a step into it, you won't go anywhere. You can be completely convinced that you need God, but until you surrender and put your faith in Him, you will not go anywhere either.

This principle applies to more than just our salvation, although that is the first step towards becoming Poor in Spirit, which a Christian will face. They must acknowledge their dependency on God for salvation and then accept that salvation. But as we mature and desire to honor God with more of our lives, we encounter many additional lessons on becoming Poor in Spirit. God reveals to us the things we need to surrender to serve Him more effectively. He shows us that when we depend on Him, He will honor that submission.

This is the blessing of becoming Poor in Spirit. The acknowledgment that we need God prepares us for submission. As we begin to shed ownership of earthly things and attitudes, we develop a closer bond with our Heavenly Father through the faith that we then acquire.

These lessons are not always easy, however, and I think sometimes we get stuck in the lobby—afraid to get on the elevator in a certain area of our lives. We have acknowledged our need for God in that area, and we just have not mustered up the strength or courage, or discipline to give it to Him. We are still fighting for some control of it or trying to claim ownership with pride.

But once we have been convicted and shown the thing that we must give up—then we must give it up! Otherwise, our progress in serving God is stalled. We may continue to make progress in other areas, but our overall impact in serving God will not reach its full potential. God wants our faith to be deepened so that we will grow in closer fellowship with Him.

So herein lies the challenge: this week, ask God to show you which area of your life you need to surrender ownership to Him—and then take steps towards doing it. Maybe it's a broad category, or perhaps a particular situation you currently face. Perhaps you don't even need to ask God to show you because you have been standing outside of that elevator for a while now. Go ahead and follow this process:

1. Identify what you are holding ownership of that needs to be given to God. Finances, a decision, time, your reputation, children, a bad habit, physical health, dreams, ambitions, a ministry, etc. What are you trying to own instead of a steward?

2. Admit to yourself the reasons that you haven't given it up yet. If you are convicted to give something to God, what is holding you back? Fear, pride, fleshly desires, etc., can all prevent us from genuinely surrendering something. Ask God to strengthen your conviction so that the call to surrender becomes more urgent than ownership of the things you are clinging to.

3. Tell someone, or at least speak it out loud. Shed light on the situation by speaking it. The Enemy wants your struggle to remain in darkness—and stay there. But the Enemy loses its foothold when we bring our struggles to the light!

4. Follow the fear—or whatever is holding you back. What's the worst you think will happen if you give up ownership of this thing? Think through your worst-case scenario of what you think might happen if you surrender. Do you believe God is still good in that scenario? Will He have failed you? No! Ask Him to help you trust in His faithfulness.

5. Let it go. Tell God that you are relinquishing ownership. Tell Him that you trust Him. Praise Him for His past faithfulness.

6. Repeat the process as frequently as needed! Submission is usually not a "one and done" deal. As situations change, or even as our day develops, we might need to repeat the submission process. It is tempting for us to snatch back control if we suddenly begin to feel afraid again or if our ego is stoked by success. Or if we desire comfort over obedience. When you feel yourself reaching for ownership, repeat this process, so you remain a steward, Poor in Spirit—available for God to use.

Dear Lord, thank you for this day. Thank you for another day where we are dependent upon you regardless of if we acknowledge it or not. You have hung this planet in its perfect place and given us air, food, and water. You have set in motion the weather, seasons, and tides. Nothing is outside your control. Let us remember that although we may try to retain ownership of things from you, everything truly is yours already. Help our faith to deepen, so we loosen the grip we have on certain things. Let us offer them up to you in love and not fear. Please bless our obedience and show us how you multiply these blessings even in the simple things we are willing to hand over to you. In Jesus' Name, Amen!

8

Poor in Spirit: Conclusion

"Blessed are the poor in spirit, for theirs is the kingdom of heaven."
Matthew 5:3

After diving in and meditating on "poor in spirit," I can't help but come to a deeper appreciation for the frequently told "loaves and fishes" story. The little boy gave up ownership of what he held, and because he gave up ownership, it was multiplied exponentially. The little boy could have had a generous heart and shared his meal with the people immediately around him, which would have been nice. However, when it was given first to Jesus, the impact the meal had was far more significant than its original potential. Likewise, we can retain ownership of what we have and do very noble things with it. But allowing God to take control provides for a more impactful legacy than we could have arranged on our own. What an important thing to keep in mind as we strive to surrender everything over to Him!

Here is a summary of what we have reflected upon during this Beatitude:

- To be Poor in Spirit means to be wholly dependent on God.
- Gideon showed us what it means to be entirely reliant on God—and he was able to accomplish great things with God's help. However, at the end of Gideon's story, we see that when he no longer thought he needed God's help, he and his family began to idolize other things. His legacy was tarnished because he no longer had the attitude of being Poor in Spirit.
- The greatest enemy of poverty is ownership! If we strive to be dependent on God and remain dependent on Him, we must seek to be stewards instead of owners of what He has allowed us to use—staying connected to Him as our provision gives us more ability to serve and honor Him with our lives.

- George Muller voluntarily depended on God in every aspect of his life. His legacy is one of great faith and miraculous provision. His faith was continually tested and therefore deepened. When we are determined to be Poor in Spirit and remain connected to God, just imagine how God can bless your faith!
- Acknowledging that we need God is only part of the battle. We must truly surrender in order to allow God to strengthen our faith and work through us.

As Christians, we have already surrendered our souls to gain salvation. However, once we begin our Christian walk, we discover many more things we need to relinquish ownership of to strengthen our faith. The more we get closer and closer to God, the more dependent on Him we become. I think that is why Jesus said that the Poor in Spirit are blessed. The poorer we become, the more reliant on God we become. And because we walk more and more by faith—surrendering earthly things—we serve Him more and more with our lives. Our faith and stewardship lead to the Kingdom of Heaven—both in eternal life and earthly life.

> *"For the kingdom of God is not a matter of eating and drinking, but of righteousness, peace and joy in the Holy Spirit,"* **Romans 14:17**

> *"'Once, on being asked by the Pharisees when the kingdom of God would come, Jesus replied, "The coming of the kingdom of God is not something that can be observed, nor will people say, 'Here it is,' or 'There it is,' because the Kingdom of God is in your midst.""* **Luke 17:20-21**

The Kingdom of Heaven, also sometimes referred to as the Kingdom of God, can be difficult to understand—the disciples even had difficulty grasping it. But ultimately, wherever God reigns, there is His Kingdom. He is the obvious ruler of Heaven, but when we allow Him to reign in our lives, His Kingdom is in us. Being Poor in Spirit prepares our hearts to receive this kingdom. And we are blessed with the privilege to carry it.

To think and pray about:

1. What do you think the Kingdom of God looks like (or should look like) here on Earth? Do you have any scriptural basis for it?
2. Do you think the Kingdom of God is evident in your life? Why or why not?

3. As we have meditated on the "blessed are the Poor in Spirit" verse, do you feel like you have made any progress in an area you've been convicted to surrender? Think of a practical way to keep working on this even as we move on to study other things.

Dear Lord, thank you for being trustworthy. Thank you for being faithful. Thank you for being all-knowing and all-powerful. Thank you for being a God that we CAN depend on. Thank you for being patient while we learn the lessons in more profound ways. Send your Kingdom to us. Help us to receive it and live it out. We love you, Lord. In Jesus' Name, Amen!

Sections 9 – 14

Mourn

9

Mourn: Definition

"Blessed are those who mourn, for they will be comforted." **Matthew 5:4**

This Beatitude, on a surface level, is my least favorite. Or at least the one I feel is most random and illogical compared to the rest of the list. The other Beatitudes seem to indicate character traits that Jesus is calling desirable. To be in mourning is not a desirable thing, nor is it part of someone's character. It is circumstantial and usually temporary, and it certainly isn't something we should strive to do—looking for things to lose and then be sad about!

So yes, this verse does not seem like an easy one to tackle and apply to our lives. However, God is so good and gracious that He provides all the inspiration and wisdom we need to tackle anything He wants us to understand! We can lean into Him in happiness or sadness and trust that He will sustain and guide us.

Jesus said, "Blessed are those who mourn." While mourning may not feel like a blessing, He said it, and therefore it must be true. But why? Mourning involves loss. To mourn is to express grief over lost potential. If someone we love dies, we might mourn because the potential to spend time with them is gone. Also, their potential to impact those around them is gone; if we lose a job, we might mourn the loss of potential to provide income, continue doing something important, or interact with our previous coworkers. If we are in mourning because of our health, we might mourn the fact that we no longer have the potential to do things we had enjoyed or planned.

Regardless of our specific source of mourning, the ultimate reason we have something to mourn for is sin. If not for sin, there would be nothing to mourn! If not for sin, we would live in a world free of death, disease, and hardship. But, living in a fallen world, we have a steady stream of disappointments and hurts to mourn.

Everyone is entitled to mourn their heartaches. But as Christians, we are also compelled to mourn the fact that sin has caused separation from the God who created us. This remembrance should evoke an emotional response as we understand the terrible consequence of sin. God himself has an emotional response to sin, so we should be no different.

To have something to mourn for is not the blessing. But when a Christ-follower mourns, they have the opportunity also to remember the big picture of sin and God's love. They have the opportunity to remember God's perspective on sin.

Ephesians 4:30 says, "And do not grieve the Holy Spirit of God..." after a passage that lists instructions on how to live as Christians and not sin. The implication is that sin causes the Trinity to grieve or mourn. And why does sin cause God to mourn? Isaiah 59:2 says, "But your iniquities have separated you from your God..." and Romans 6:23 says, "For the wages of sin is death..." Many verses in the Bible testify that sin has created a barrier between God and us. Since God created us and loves us so much, it is no wonder that He would mourn! As His children, when we stop to think about this entire salvation story, we should also be compelled to mourn.

To think and pray about:

1. Think about something you have mourned about before or something you currently mourn. Did that situation and emotional response eventually draw you closer to God?

2. When you think of sin—yours or the sins of others—how does it make you feel? If you haven't given it much thought before, allow yourself to realize the true significance of sin and its consequences.

3. Read Isaiah 59—the entire chapter. It steps through the whole process of sin, justice, and redemption. Is there any particular verse that you feel you should meditate further on?

Dear Lord, thank you for giving us a way to recognize the pain of sin so that we can have a better appreciation for the redemption story. Thank you for loving us enough that you rescue us from our self-destructive sin. Thank you for your patience with us, as we sometimes take a while to repent of it. Please help us to develop a deeper understanding of what it means to mourn with you over sin. And please give us comfort as we face our individual pains to mourn. In Jesus' Name, Amen!

10

Mourn: Biblical Example

"Blessed are those who mourn, for they will be comforted." **Matthew 5:4**

To mourn, as previously discussed, is to grieve a loss. We grieve because we live in a sinful world full of the consequences of sin. As Christians, we mourn not in despair but in acknowledgment of these consequences and the pain they cause.

"Jesus wept." **John 11:35**

We know this because Jesus wept. The context of John 11:35 is that Jesus had returned to the home of Mary, Martha, and Lazarus just after Lazarus had died. Jesus mourned the loss of his friend even though He knew the end of the story. Jesus was about to raise Lazarus from the dead. He grieved for the pain of Mary and Martha, even though He knew it was temporary. He wept for the lost time where Lazarus had been in the grave, even though Jesus knew that everything would be redeemed. But most of all, He mourned because of the need for redemption.

To ignore the need for redemption and not to mourn is to cheapen everything that Jesus did for us. Jesus did not weep because of His impending victory—He wept because sin caused the need for His sacrifice. He wept because of the chasm that sin created between God and man—even though it was a chasm He was capable of bridging.

There is so much freedom in seeing that Jesus wept. The fact that His hope and victory did not diminish His urge to mourn sets the example for us to follow. We all have things to mourn—sometimes small and sometimes big. We do not need to feel guilt for these undesirable emotions—experiencing them leads to blessing. When we grieve, despite our hope, we honor God by acknowledging His redemptive plan for our lives and for humanity. Our grief should then remind us that Jesus has already overcome sin and death, and that brings us comfort.

> *"We all, like sheep, have gone astray, each of us has turned to our own way, and the Lord has laid on him the iniquity of us all."* **Isaiah 53:6**

Our grief should also remind us that we have sinned. It is easy to say "we live in a fallen world" or "because the serpent tempted Eve...," but we each have succumbed to sin as well. It is a humbling thing indeed to think that Jesus paid the price for my personal sins. For your personal sins. For the sins of our families. The sins of our friends. The sins of our enemies. All of these were His burden to bear in order to save us.

So Jesus wept. Jesus mourned the loss of His own life, even when He knew He would regain it. He mourned the necessity of the price He must pay. He mourned because each of our sins needed to be covered with His blood. And because every sin ever committed was covered in His blood and redeemed, the consequences of those sins were also redeemed.

Every time we experience pain and heartbreak from living in this fallen world, we must remember that Jesus' blood has already redeemed the sins that led to our pain. That does not negate the pain—we should still mourn—but we do not despair. Instead, we honor His sacrifice by mourning and allow it to draw us closer to the loving God who made salvation possible.

To think and pray about:

1. Hebrews 5:7-10 says, "During the days of Jesus' life on Earth, he offered up prayers and petitions with fervent cries and tears to the one who could save him from death, and he was heard because of his reverent submission. Son though he was, he learned obedience from what he suffered and, once made perfect, he became the Source of eternal salvation for all who obey him and was designated by God to be high priest in the order of Melchizedek." Jesus, while mourning his future sacrifice, learned obedience from what He suffered. Interestingly, Jesus had to *learn* obedience—He didn't have a DNA tweak that made obedience compulsory. Also, it wasn't His sin that taught Him this obedience. Has your suffering or pain (regardless of whose sin caused it) brought you lessons of obedience? Is there a time when maybe it should have?

2. Have you ever directly mourned the sin in your life? Not the consequences, but the actual acts of disobedience themselves? Does remembering that Jesus paid the penalty make it easier to mourn?

3. Read Isaiah 53. It outlines, in great detail, the suffering that Jesus went through on our behalf. As a way to keep meditating on this lesson, listen to the song "By His Wounds," which was inspired by this chapter.

Dear Lord, thank you for loving us enough to send your son to die for us. Thank you for the example Jesus set so that we have permission to mourn, even though you have filled us with hope. Thank you for being patient as we learn more about obedience. Show us how to honor you by mourning sin, but keep us from despair. Protect us from the lies of the Enemy that tell us we do not deserve hope, and instead, let us remember the price you paid for us. We love you, Lord. In Jesus' Name, Amen!

11

Mourn: Stumbling Blocks

"Blessed are those who mourn, for they will be comforted." **Matthew 5:4**

What frequently stops us from mourning? Hope. Whether it is hope bubbling up from within our hearts, or hope being pushed on us from well-meaning Christians, hope often suppresses or stops the mourning process. Why should we mourn when we have hope? In some ways, it feels disrespectful to God to mourn the death of someone we know is now in Heaven and at peace or ungrateful to bemoan our health problems when He has promised us that He will provide all the strength we need. Or foolish to mourn our disappointments when we have the promise that God uses all these things for our good and His glory.

We may feel guilty when torn between hope and mourning. Our friends might try to comfort us in our grief—reminding us of hope so that we will no longer feel sad. Or Christian leaders may gently reprimand the body of Christ with verses of hope, hope, and more hope! And it's great to have hope and be reminded of all these scriptures! What a wonderful thing hope is!

It is tempting to skip the mourning and go straight to hope, but it cheapens the victory if we do not acknowledge the sacrifice made to get there. Blessed are those who mourn. Jesus didn't say, "Blessed are those who don't feel the need to mourn because they have hope." Hope and mourning can coexist. Jesus' example is proof of that. Hopeful mourning may seem counter-intuitive, but in reality, it is extremely powerful.

Hopeful mourning brings about a heart of more profound gratitude than hope alone could ever bring. Hopeful mourning strengthens our faith more than hope alone could ever do. Hopeful mourning reminds us that not only is God all-powerful and in control, but He also has skin in the game. It reminds us of His limitless love.

When sin was unleashed into the world, a new portion of God's character was unlocked for us to experience. Compassion, mercy, patience: these things are not necessary in a sinless and perfect world. So, while the Enemy intended sin to separate us from God, God is so great that it allowed for Him to be shown more gloriously radiant. This is such a huge deal—but we shouldn't just skip over all the bad that came before the good. We appreciate these things about God, along with redemption, all the more when we mourn the brokenness of the world.

We mourn the existence of sin and death. We mourn while simultaneously holding onto hope, with neither hoping nor mourning diminishing the other. We thank God for the parts of His character that we get to access due to our imperfect world. And we marvel at the intricacy of how He works everything together.

To think and pray about:

1. Have you ever tried to brush aside mourning and go straight to hoping instead? Did it make you feel better, or did you feel like you were missing out on the emotions of mourning?

2. Compassion, mercy, patience: What other parts of God's character do we get to experience as a result of sin? Thank God for these traits!

3. Has mourning ever made you feel guilty? Remember that even Jesus mourned while having hope, so being sad does not mean you are ungrateful or have less faith. We can (and should) mourn even while full of hope.

Dear Lord, thank you for this day. Thank you for the hope that you have given us because of your love and redemption. Thank you for your patience and kindness, and mercy. Please help us to better understand his balance of mourning sin and still having hope. Please allow us to feel the weight of the sacrifice you made while also being able to have joy and faith. Let this dichotomy of emotions become something we can practice daily so that we can develop an even more profound gratitude for who you are and what you have done. In Jesus' Name, Amen.

12

Mourn: Modern Example

"Blessed are those who mourn, for they will be comforted." **Matthew 5:4**

"No, in all these things, we are more than conquerors through Him who loved us. For I am convinced that neither death nor life, neither angels nor demons, neither the present nor the future, nor any powers, neither height nor depth, nor anything else in all creation, will be able to separate us from the love of God that is in Christ Jesus our Lord." **Romans 8:37-39**

When preparing to write about a modern example of someone who exemplified "blessed are those who mourn," only one name came to mind: Corrie Ten Boom. Corrie was a woman from Holland who survived the Holocaust. Her story is incredible, and the ways God used her are miraculous. However, she lost so much that she loved it in the process. Her family hid Jews from the Nazis, and they continued doing so until they were arrested. Corrie's father and sister, Betsie, died in prison camps.

During World War II, Corrie Ten Boom had many things to mourn. Life-altering circumstances, miserable discomforts, and the deaths of the people most precious to her. She had so much grief, so many hardships. Yet, all of these things were used to deepen her faith and spur her on to serving God even more. The terrible things she experienced were redeemed, and she continually gave God the glory and thanks for getting her through.

Before the war and the arrests and prison camps, Corrie experienced heartbreak. The man that she loved married another woman because of pressure from his family. Corrie was left crushed because of it. In her autobiography, The Hiding Place, Corrie recalls the counsel her father gave to her:

> "Corrie," he began instead, "do you know what hurts so very much? It's love. Love is the strongest force in the world, and when it is blocked that means pain.
>
> "There are two things we can do when this happens. We can kill the love so that it stops hurting. But then of course part of us dies, too. Or, Corrie, we can ask God to open up another route for that love to travel.
>
> "God loves Karel—even more than you do—and if you ask Him, He will give you *His* love for this man, a love nothing can prevent, nothing destroy. Whenever we cannot love in the old, human way, Corrie, God can give us His perfect way."
>
> I did not know, as I listened to Father's footsteps winding back down the stairs, that he had given me more than the key to this hard moment. I did not know that he had put into my hands the secret that would open far darker rooms than this—places where there was not, on a human level, anything to love at all.

Corrie learned that in tragic circumstances, God would give us what we need if we ask Him. She leaned on that truth over and over again, and God provided in His perfect way. And she learned that shutting out the mournful feelings was not the way to be strong—it was the path to spiritual death. Ignoring the pain, or killing it, leads to part of us dying too. Corrie says, in her book, "I saw that stony indifference to others that was the most fatal disease of the concentration camp." When people were so tired of mourning their personal heartaches, they became indifferent to everyone else around them. They killed the love that they had instead of asking God to redirect it.

But Corrie, while she was in a concentration camp with Betsie, allowed God to redirect her love as He saw fit. The Ten Boom sisters had been (miraculously) able to smuggle a Bible into their barracks, and they began leading worship services for the other women. Despite everything they went through, they were shining examples of Jesus' love in a dark place. She wrote:

> "It grew harder and harder. Even within these four walls there was too much misery, too much seemingly pointless suffering. Every day something else failed to make sense, something else grew too heavy. "Will You carry this too, Lord Jesus?"

"But as the rest of the world grew stranger, one thing became increasingly clear. And that was the reason the two of us were here. Why others should suffer we were not shown. As for us, from morning until lights-out, whenever we were not in ranks for roll call, our Bible was the center of an ever-widening circle of help and hope. Like waifs clustered around a blazing fire, we gathered about it, holding out our hearts to its warmth and light. The blacker the night around us grew, the brighter and truer and more beautiful burned the word of God. "Who shall separate us from the love of Christ? Shall tribulation, or distress, or persecution, or famine, or nakedness, or peril, or sword?... Nay, in all these things we are more than conquerors through him that loved us."

"I would look about us as Betsie read, watching the light leap from face to face. More than conquerors. It was not a wish. It was a fact. We knew it, we experienced it minute by minute—poor, hated, hungry. We are more than conquerors. Not "we shall be." We are! Life in Ravensbruck took place on two separate levels, mutually impossible. One, the observable, external life, grew every day more horrible. The other, the life we lived with God, grew daily better, truth upon truth, glory upon glory.

"Sometimes I would slip the Bible from its little sack with hands that shook, so mysterious had it become to me. It was new; it had just been written. I marveled sometimes that the ink was dry. I had believed the Bible always, but reading it now had nothing to do with belief. It was simply a description of the way things were—of hell and heaven, of how men act and how God acts. I had read a thousand times the story of Jesus' arrest—how soldiers had slapped Him, laughed at Him, flogged Him. Now such happenings had faces and voices."

Wow. Such peace and clarity and wisdom Corrie received in the middle of terrible circumstances! God used her and Betsie to serve others around them because they made themselves available for His purposes. Up until she died, Betsie continued to radiate God's love for His people and to inspire Corrie to do the same. After Corrie was released from the prison camp, she continued to minister to others and share the wisdom she had learned.

What a testimony Corrie had! Amid her mourning, God performed many miracles of provision and peace. She developed a deeper appreciation for the

Word of God and the suffering of Jesus. There are so many lessons we can learn from her story! But if she had closed herself off from feeling and become indifferent to it all, she would not have been an available conduit for God to use.

To think and pray about:

1. Is there a circumstance in your life where you have tried to suppress or kill love instead of asking God to redirect it? Perhaps someone died, left your life, or hurt you. Or possibly doors were closed on a path you were passionate about. Ask God to give you His perfect way to love in that situation so that you see another route for that love to travel.

2. Have you ever experienced, or watch someone else experience, seemingly pointless suffering? Don't let your heart be hardened to it. Take refuge in the words of the Bible. Ask God to shed His light and show His purpose.

3. We are more than conquerors. 'Are,' not will be. Is there a part of your life where you need to claim this promise?

Dear Lord, thank you for this day. Thank you for the opportunity we have to reflect on your love for us in the midst of suffering and mourning. Thank you for being victorious over all the battles we must face. Thank you for providing purposeful outlets for the love that spills over in our hearts from you. Guide this love and passion in the way that you see fit so that our disappointments and losses end up being blessed redirections. May we learn to keep loving in our mourning so that we are more and more like Jesus. In Jesus' Name, Amen!

13

Mourn: Challenge

"Blessed are those who mourn, for they will be comforted." **Matthew 5:4**

"Godly sorrow brings repentance that leads to salvation and leaves no regret, but worldly sorrow brings death." **2 Corinthians 7:10**

Did you know there was a difference in sorrows? When we mourn, we have a choice—Godly sorrow or worldly sorrow. The verse says Godly sorrow brings repentance while worldly sorrow brings death. Obviously, as Christians, we want to choose Godly sorrow, but how?

Godly sorrow that leads to repentance and salvation must be centered around Jesus' pain, whereas worldly sorrow is centered around the pain of self. Basically, when someone is filled with Godly sorrow, they acknowledge that sin in the world created a separation between God and man—requiring Jesus' sacrifice. Godly sorrow does not negate the personal pain we feel but rather draws us closer to God because we know He feels the pain too. We mourn with Him and He with us.

Worldly sorrow centers around self. It is like a pity party. It is empty and isolating. It leads to death because it never brings about the acknowledgment of our need for God. Worldly sorrow is not shared sorrow between God and us—we solely carry it.

Do you have something to mourn? Has your sin, or the sin of someone else, caused you grief? Are your expectations for this season of life not lining up with its reality? Have you lost something or someone? Maybe it's a current situation, or perhaps it's something from the past that still hurts. "Blessed are those who mourn," so go ahead and mourn!

This week, choose something—past or present—that has caused you sorrow. Then decide to mourn it with Godly sorrow. Choose to remember that Jesus died for the sins that led up to that situation. Choose to recognize that you are not alone in your grief. Choose to look for redemption in the grief. Then ask God to give you the comfort that He has promised.

To think and pray about:

1. In recent weeks we read Isaiah 53 and 59, both of which outlined Jesus' suffering. This week read Isaiah 61, which talks about the Lord's favor. Which of the verses stand out to you?

2. Isaiah 61:3 talks about getting a "garment of praise instead of a spirit of despair." Worship will definitely help us to refocus away from ourselves and back onto God. Try to find a hymn or worship song to get stuck in your head!

3. Can you think of a time when you have chosen worldly sorrow instead of Godly? Did you find comfort in it? Were you eventually able to switch worldly sorrow for Godly?

Dear Lord, thank you for your Word. Thank you for the guidance and wisdom you provide through it at just the right timing. Thank you for being a faithful God who mourns alongside us. Please help us to learn how to approach our sorrows in a way that honors you. Let us be blessed through our mourning. In Jesus' Name, Amen.

14

Mourn: Conclusion

"Blessed are those who mourn, for they will be comforted." **Matthew 5:4**

Even still, after six weeks of study and meditation, this verse seems out of place amongst the other Beatitudes. However, I've started to see the value of it. Mourning, godly mourning, serves to bring us closer to God. And what more of a blessing is there?

Here's a summary of what we have reflected on during this Beatitude:

- To mourn is to grieve lost potential. The ultimate reason we mourn is because of sin in the world.

- Jesus himself mourned, even though He knew the end of the story. Mourning reminds us of the sacrifices Jesus made for us and the fact He died for each and every sin. We can honor Jesus' sacrifice through mourning the reasons that He died.

- We must be careful not to skip over mourning and go straight to hope. Instead, we should mourn while having hope.

- Corrie Ten Boom was a great example of what it can look like to experience complete heartache while still pursuing God's purpose in the middle of the mess. Through her faith in the trials, she encouraged so many people that were placed in her path.

- Not all mourning is beneficial and blessed. 2 Corinthians 7:10 tells the difference between godly sorrow and worldly sorrow. When we mourn the painful situations in our lives, we must remember to mourn in the way that draws us nearer to God, not in the way that isolates us from Him.

It seems that the blessing of comfort Jesus refers to is that mourning draws us closer to God. When people go through tragedies together, there is a natural bond that can form between them. Similarly, when we go through our personal heartaches and remember to include God in our mourning, our bond with Him is strengthened. We are closer to Him, and we are comforted.

> *"The Lord is close to the brokenhearted and saves those who are crushed in spirit."*
> *-Psalm 34:18*

Jesus said we are blessed when we mourn; the Psalmist says we are closer to God, and He saves us. Maybe the Beatitude makes some sense after all! Like Corrie Ten Boom, whose faith and walk with the Lord was sweeter each day in the prison camp, perhaps true blessing comes to us when we keep the Heavenly perspective on our Earthly mourning. The suffering is temporary. None of it negates or changes God's character. And He will supply us with joy afterward.

> *"For his anger lasts only a moment, but his favor lasts a lifetime; weeping may stay for the night, but rejoicing comes in the morning."* *-Psalm 30:5*

The Bible is full of promises about our grief being temporary. We do not need to despair, even in our most painful moments. Nor should we ignore the pain, thinking that it will make us stronger. When we acknowledge our need to grieve and see how sin has created brokenness in the world, we will find comfort in our nearness to God. We can then begin to experience the truth of Jesus' words.

To think and pray about:

1. What other verses can you think of that give us a promise of comfort from God? Think of a way to make them easily accessible to your memory in times of grief.

2. Read Psalm 30 and Psalm 34. In both of these, David has been experiencing intense trouble in his life. However, take note that he begins both Psalms with praise! He doesn't ignore the pain he has been feeling; however, beginning with praise reminds him to have a proper perspective. When you start thinking or praying about the troubles you face, follow David's example and start with praise!

3. Is there someone you know who is going through a period of mourning? How can you encourage them in a way that brings about the balance of hopeful mourning instead of only hope or hopeless mourning?

Amy M. Blindt

Dear Lord, thank you for your words. Thank you for your Heavenly logic, which so often does not line up with our earthly logic. Thank you for being patient with us as we try to figure it all out. Lord, in this challenging time we face, please help us to have your Heavenly perspective as well. Let us be quick to worship, but in a profound way that does not ignore any pain we feel. Please help us to have that balance that only you can provide. We love you, Lord. In Jesus' Name, Amen.

Sections 15 – 20

Meek

15

Meek: Definition

*"Blessed are the Meek, for they will inherit the earth." -**Matthew 5:5***

"Meek" is not a word I hear used very often, but when I do, it's often used in either an incomplete or negative context. Mild, patient, humble, passive, weak, gentle, submissive, etc., are all ways that meekness is described today. In our current society, for the most part, these are not characteristics of one who is successful or admirable. They are perceived weaknesses.

However, the Greek origin of "Meek" is "praus." It was a very complimentary word in Ancient Greece and was used to describe war horses. These horses were tamed and trained—their "strength under authority." Their "power under control."

That seems to be where our current society gets meekness wrong: we stop at the surface layer. On the surface, meekness may look like passivity, submissiveness, or weakness. If a war horse is acting mild and calm because of signals from his master, its strength is not revealed. But really, their strength is being reined in. The horse is far from weak—in fact, the self-control makes them even more powerful than an untamed horse with a similar muscle build.

Someone who is biblically Meek is similarly strong, even though their surface demeanor may be calm. It isn't weakness or fear—it is restraint. It is the obedience to the convictions of God's timing and God's ways. Meekness is being available to act when God says "act!" but being okay with waiting. I appreciate this commentary:

> *"Meekness is therefore an active and deliberate acceptance of undesirable circumstances that are wisely seen by the individual as only part of a larger picture. Meekness is not a resignation to fate, a passive and reluctant submission to events,*

for there is little virtue in such a response. Nevertheless, since the two responses—resignation and meekness are externally often indistinguishable, it is easy to see how what was once perceived as a virtue has become a defect in contemporary society. The patient and hopeful endurance of undesirable circumstances identifies the person as externally vulnerable and weak but inwardly resilient and strong. Meekness does not identify the weak but more precisely the strong who have been placed in a position of weakness where they persevere without giving up."

So when Jesus encouraged meekness with His statement, He was encouraging strength in our obedience to our Master. He was encouraging the taming of our potential so that it can be used for God's glory instead of our self-interests. He was encouraging us to seek God's timing in place of our impulsive timing.

Jesus Himself showed meekness. He remained silent when insulted. He appeared passive when accused of crimes. He was submissive to those who flailed Him and nailed Him to the cross. Was He without strength during these trials? No! His strength was reined in, understanding that His momentary suffering was part of a larger purpose. His patience showed Him to be resilient—not weak. Or what about when Jesus was tempted in the desert? He had the power to end the temptations, yet He chose to endure meekly.

Let us begin to gain an understanding of how we can be meek in our spiritual walks.

To think and pray about:

1. Finish reading this commentary (it's not super long, I promise) https://www.biblestudytools.com/dictionary/meekness/. Is there anything else about meekness that stands out to you?

2. In what aspects of your life are you tamed and meek? In what situations do you struggle with meekness? Ask God to help you identify the areas you need to become a warhorse instead of a wild horse.

3. What is a practical way you can remind yourself to be reined in? Is there a scripture, hymn, etc., that you can meditate on to help?

Dear Lord, thank you for the lesson of meekness. Thank you for showing us the importance of restraint and the value of following your timing. Help us to forgo our impulsive responses to undesirable situations and instead look to you for guidance and insight. Help us to recognize the ways you use our opportunities for Meekness as opportunities for refinement as we allow our character to be shaped by you. We love you, Lord. In Jesus' Name, Amen.

16

Meek: Biblical Example

*"Blessed are the Meek, for they will inherit the earth." -**Matthew 5:5***

Meekness—such a misunderstood virtue in today's culture! Fortunately, we can look to the Bible for examples of what it means to be meek. To be meek is to trust in God's timing above our own. To be meek is to exhibit self-control--doing the right thing and not the impulsive thing. To be meek is to be strong and capable while yielding to God's authority.

1 Samuel 25 tells the story of Abigail--a strong, intelligent, and also meek woman. King David, before he was king, was in the wilderness with his men. They were staying near the workers of a very wealthy man named Nabal. David's men treated the workers well and did not make any trouble for them, so David sent a message to Nabal, asking for favor and food. Nabal, who the Bible describes as "surly and mean," rudely rejected David's request. David was infuriated by the insult and decided to attack Nabal's household.

Abigail, Nabal's wife, heard about the situation. She immediately gathered a bunch of food as a peace offering and went to meet David. When she came up to him on the path, she got off her donkey and humbly spoke to him. She apologized on behalf of her husband and spoke many blessings over David. David responded positively and decided to spare Nabal because of her actions:

> *"Then David accepted from her hand what she had brought him and said, "Go home in peace. I have heard your words and granted your request." When Abigail went to Nabal, he was in the house holding a banquet like that of a king. He was in high spirits and very drunk. So she told him nothing at all until daybreak. Then in the morning, when Nabal was sober, his wife told him all these things, and his*

heart failed him, and he became like a stone. About ten days later, the Lord struck Nabal, and he died." ***1 Samuel 25:35-38***

We see in this story how Abigail acted with meek strength. From a worldly perspective, she had every right to treat her husband with contempt and anger, yet she didn't. Some things we can learn from Abigail's story:

- When Abigail heard about the problems Nabal was causing, she immediately sought to fix the situation. She didn't first go to Nabal and complain about how he was causing her more work--she just took the initiative and fixed the problem. She didn't even tell him that she was going; she knew what was right, and so she did it. She didn't need to explain or justify her actions; Abigail did what was right, simply because it was right.

- Abigail could have chosen to do nothing when she heard about David's anger towards Nabal. She could have let him "get what was coming to him," but that wouldn't have been meekness; it would have been a weakness. Abigail shows us that being meek truly means reining our personal interests instead of acting nobly for God. She knew that a wife's duty is not to ignore a husband's foolishness nor participate in it. She could still do right in a way that was not disrespectful to her husband, so she found a way.

- After Abigail got home from speaking with David, she saw that Nabal was drunk. She had the opportunity to angrily rebuke him at that time--but she didn't. She waited until the next day to tell him of the situation.

The story of Abigail shows how meekness involves showing restraint and doing the right things in the right times. When it was time for her to act and take food to David--she did immediately. When it came to talking to Nabal about everything that occurred, she waited until the right time. She was also more interested in doing what was right, than in explaining or justifying what she was doing. God ended up punishing Nabal--it was not for David or Abigail to do.

I think one of our biggest tests of meekness involves our interactions with others--especially the people we interact with on a regular basis. When someone around us is acting foolishly, irresponsibly, unkindly, etc. we have the power to choose our response to the situation. A meek response is focused on what is godly--not one that is full of self-interest. A meek response is confidently humble--unconcerned with explaining and proving oneself to others. A meek response is also bold enough to act when the Lord prompts but patient enough to wait for that prompting. Abigail sets such an excellent example for us to follow!

To think and pray about:

1. Read 1 Samuel 25. What else stands out to you with how Abigail approached the volatile situation?

2. Is there a recurring situation in your life where you should be learning meekness? Perhaps a child who is caught in a specific cycle of disobedience. Perhaps a spouse who has a habit that causes you frustration or annoyance. Perhaps a friend, neighbor, or coworker who inadvertently causes you extra work. How do you think Abigail would respond? Think through how you can approach this situation with more meekness the next time you are faced with it.

3. Think about the different combined characteristics to create meekness: strength, patience, honor, self-control, and subservience. Are there any of these that you feel influential in? Any that you struggle with? Ask God to help balance out your character so that you can learn to approach more and more situations with meekness.

Dear Lord, thank you for the story of Abigail. Thank you for giving us such a great example of someone who exhibited the strength of meekness. Thank you for showing us how You redeem these situations and claim justice per your will and not our own. Please help us to learn to trust you with the troublesome situations in our lives. Help us to learn to approach them with meekness so that we do not inflame them further. Let us continually keep in mind that we have a responsibility to do what is right, regardless of the decisions of those around us. Help us to surrender our expectations so that we have the patience to wait on you. We love you, Lord. In Jesus' Name, Amen!

17

Meek: Stumbling Blocks

*"Blessed are the Meek, for they will inherit the earth." -**Matthew 5:5***

The other week I went grocery shopping. That's a pretty regular chore, but the circumstances of life during Covid were not normal! I had a shopping list for my own family, a list from my parents, and a list from a friend. I was just trying to help and serve others where I could. As I went through the store, my cart kept getting more and more packed. The fuller it got, the more self-conscious I became. *Do the other customers think I'm panic buying? Do they think I'm a food hoarder???*

I couldn't help but have these thoughts go through my mind—expecting judgment even though I wasn't doing anything wrong! It was tempting to constantly tell the other customers that I was shopping for more than one family. Or point out that I only had 1 gallon of milk. Or inform them that I have nine people living in my house!

I checked out, and the woman bagging my groceries (they wouldn't let me do it) had to get creative with stacking the bags into the cart--but she made it work. The self-consciousness reached its' peak as I strolled out of the grocery store with an overflowing cart, passing by the line of people who were waiting to get in. *Does everyone think I've wasted their time by taking too long in the store??? Do they think I got all the "good groceries" and left nothing for them?*

The experience made me realize that one of the biggest stumbling blocks for meekness is pride. This aspect of pride makes us want to justify our actions of obedience so that people aren't mistaking our meekness for weakness. This pride also makes us is harder for us to submit to the will of God instead of the will of our flesh. This pride instills in us a desire to be right instead of a desire to be righteous.

Meekness is internal, just as pride is. It is a posture of the heart. Because of that, no one sees our meekness! (Or our pride.) The external fruit of a meek heart can easily be misconstrued for other things. When we are meek, we may appear too passive, too submissive, too hesitant, too lenient, or too weak-willed. But just as we find the strength to tame our flesh to our Master's authority, we must also find the strength to tame our prideful reputation to be focused on preserving our Master's reputation instead.

The book of Romans is filled with instructions on how to live as a Christian. As we live more and more by these principles, taming our prideful flesh, I believe meekness will naturally follow. Here are some verses to stand on in those moments where meekness seems just out of grasp:

- If I am trying to be meek, but am worried about how people might misconstrue my actions:

   "Do not conform to the pattern of this world, but be transformed by the renewing of your mind. Then you will be able to test and approve what God's will is—his good, pleasing and perfect will." -**Romans 12:2**

- If I am trying to be meek but am having trouble choosing God's will over my own:

   "Those who live according to the flesh have their minds set on what the flesh desires, but those who live in accordance with the Spirit have their minds set on what the Spirit desires. The mind governed by the flesh is death, but the mind governed by the Spirit is life and peace." -**Romans 8:5-6**

- If I am trying to be meek, but am wanting to win more than I want to do what is right:

   "So I find this law at work: Although I want to do good, evil is right there with me. For in my inner being, I delight in God's law; but I see another law at work in me, waging war against the law of my mind and making me a prisoner of the law of sin at work within me. What a wretched man I am! Who will rescue me from this body that is subject to death? Thanks be to God, who delivers me through Jesus Christ our Lord!" -**Romans 7:21-25**

To think and pray about:

1. Choose one of the bullet points above that resonates the most with your struggle to be meek. Read the associated chapter in Romans (12, 8, or 7) and see what other wisdom you can glean!

2. Besides pride, is there anything else that makes meekness difficult for you? What sort of Biblical encouragement can you use to combat it?

3. To the world, meekness is not a valued characteristic. Do you value it? Do you want to be better at it? What practical steps can you take in your life right now to set yourself up for success in this area?

Dear Lord, thank you for meekness. Thank you for being a God that continually defies human logic and human values. You set yourself apart from the flesh so that we are in awe of you. Meekness is truly an internal battle—please fight for us. Please help us to die to our flesh so that you shine through us. Help us to value your approval instead of the world's. Help us to seek your will first and foremost. And help us to do what is right over what feels good in the moment. We love you, Lord. In Jesus' Name, Amen!

18

Meek: Modern Example

*"Blessed are the Meek, for they will inherit the earth." -**Matthew 5:5***

"I wish thy way.
And when in me myself should rise,
And long for something otherwise,
Then Lord, take sword and spear
And slay."
-**Amy Carmichael**

That's a pretty intense thing to say! To ask God to slay our desires that do not line up with His. But Amy Carmichael was a woman completely dedicated to God. She was His humble servant, following His leadings to serve the people He put in her path. She was strong and determined—but strong and determined when it came to the Lord's purposes, not her own. Amy was meek.

Amy was a missionary to India for over 50 years without pause. She dedicated her life to spreading the gospel and sharing Christ's love. However, it wasn't an easy mission field. She encountered much persecution and hardship because of the deep-rooted Hindu, Muslim, and Indian caste traditions. The things she accomplished could not have been done by someone who was prideful, self-centered, or self-serving. Amy defied human logic and desires—focusing only on what God would have her do.

Amy Carmichael was not a physically strong woman, so it didn't make sense that she would leave the relative comfort of Europe to live in a more physically challenging environment. But she followed her convictions anyway and lived in India for 55 years. Amy was determined to reach as many with the gospel as she could, but when God began sending unwanted children to her, she embraced this change of direction and started a children's home.

Amy was a great speaker and could have become an even greater one. However, she knew that God was calling her to minister to the children, and she gave up her opportunity for recognition to serve them. Additionally, Amy was injured in her 60s and spent her last 20 years mostly bedridden. She stayed in India and used that time to write about the things God had done and taught her in her life.

Amy was humble and completely Christ-focused. Like that image of a Greek war horse—with strength under authority—she dedicated her strength in obedience to God. She rescued girls from temple prostitution, stood up to local magistrates, and challenged Indian families to love the unwanted. But she did it all so meekly and humbly. She did it with the forceful power of Christ's love, not the forces of human desire. The things she did showed her great fortitude, but how she did them showed her meekness.

One of my favorite quotes from Amy Carmichael is, "a cup brimful of sweet water cannot spill even one drop of bitter water however suddenly jolted." Amy realized that if she was filled with Christ's love, then even the most unexpected or unpleasant circumstance would not bring forth a bitter response. While that may not seem relevant to meekness on the surface, it just goes to show that Amy was dedicated to her Master, and she knew the importance of following Him implicitly. Likewise, when we are filled with meekness—Biblical meekness—then we can remain obedient regardless of our circumstances.

To think and pray about:

1. Amy Carmichael also said: "If I am afraid to speak the truth lest I lose affection, or lest the one concerned should say, "You do not understand," or because I fear to lose my reputation for kindness; if I put my own good name before the other's highest good, then I know nothing of Calvary love." She understood that the obedience of speaking the truth has nothing to do with our own gain but about showing Christ's love through sharing the truth. Is there a circumstance in your life where you have been hesitating to share God's truth because you fear the potential personal consequences?

2. Are you determined to obey God no matter what the cost? Are you single-minded when it comes to your faith? Ask God to show you a

step you can take in that direction: to become even more meekly obedient to His calling.

3. As discussed, meekness is about humble obedience to God, looking for nothing in return. 1 Corinthians 15:58 gives us an encouraging reminder: "Therefore, my dear brothers and sisters, stand firm. Let nothing move you. Always give yourselves fully to the work of the Lord because you know that your labor in the Lord is not in vain." Meditate on that verse this week, asking God to show you what work of His He would have you do.

Dear Lord, thank you for the legacy of Amy Carmichael. Thank you for showing us, through her story, that you can use any of us if we are willing. Thank you for the example of meekness she sets for us. Her obedience to You, the Master, is both inspiring and convicting. Thank you for allowing her to write about your faithfulness in her life. Please help us to develop a deeper understanding of how we can each become meeker in our own life. Let us have the courage, in You, to do so. We love you, Lord. In Jesus' Name, Amen!

19

Meek: Challenge

*"Blessed are the Meek, for they will inherit the earth." -***Matthew 5:5**

"Strength under authority" and "power under control" is how the word "meek" was defined in its original context. I like those words: "strength" and "power"; "authority" and "control"! It makes me feel like meekness is almost a disguised fierceness—a strategic withholding to put the enemy off track. Like being a secret agent on this earth, and not showing off the strength and power I could wield.

But then there's the word "under," and it brings the whole image crashing down. You might say it *undermines* my delusions of grandeur that those definitions of meekness stir up inside of me. Because if I gloss over the word "under," I make the act of submission seem less important. Less difficult. Less of a victory. But being "under" truly makes meekness what it is.

There is no meekness without submission. And a person cannot be considered one of "THE meek" Jesus talks about without exhibiting that submissive Biblical nature as a part of who they are. To indeed be meek, we need to keep submitting more and more of our lives to God.

I think we all have areas where meekness is easy and other areas where it is more difficult. Perhaps you are very good at approaching your work with Godly meekness, but then when you speak to your family, it is apparent that your flesh wins. Perhaps you are meek with your finances, but you seek control when it comes to your time. There are many areas of our lives where we want to be in control or allow our fleshly impulses to control us. Or we fail to yield to God's authority. We will never be perfect! However, making a conscious effort to submit in a new area will bring us closer to walking in unison with Him.

This week, take a look at two areas of your life. The first should be an area where you think you are already in a posture of meekness. The second should be an area you are convicted of moving towards a posture of meekness.

To think and pray about this week:

1. What is the area of life you feel already meek? What is it that makes that area easier to submit than another?

2. What is the area of your life that you feel convicted to submit? Have you tried submitting this area in the past? What has prevented you, or what do you think might prevent you from being successful? Why do you think God is convicting you to work on this area?

3. Identify something that will motivate you or remind you to become meeker in the area you are working on—a Bible verse, a worship song, a phrase, etc. Keep meditating on the truth of that message to bring you to a new level of meekness. Ask God to help solidify the conviction, and send you help, so you will know you are on the right track.

Dear Lord, thank you for submission. Thank you for sending us examples of what it looks like—Jesus, Abigail, Amy Carmichael, and more! Thank you also for conviction—even though it is uncomfortable. I pray that you convict each of our hearts to recognize the area you would have us submit to you this week. Please give us the grace and strength and the opportunity to work on it. Thank you for your patience as we learn. We love you, Lord. In Jesus' Name, Amen!

20

Meek: Conclusion

*"Blessed are the Meek, for they will inherit the earth." -***Matthew 5:5**

To be a person of meekness is a blessing!

Here is a summary of what we have reflected on during this Beatitude:

- On the surface, a meek person often looks submissive, weak-willed, or like a pushover. However, the actual definition shows the depth and strength of a meek character. Like the visible portion of an iceberg—those characteristics only show part of the story. Unlike weakness, meekness is built on a deep foundation of faith and hope. "Strength under authority" and "power under control" are truly admirable achievements, even if no one ever understands them for what they are. God still sees!

- Abigail, in the Bible, shows us meekness in action. She was able to gracefully navigate a difficult situation due to her meek nature. She chose her responses based on what was right, not how she felt or was being treated.

- One of the natural stumbling blocks to meekness is pride. We want to be liked; we want approval; we want to make people happy; we want to do things our way, etc. These things are not bad in themselves, but when we allow them to compromise our convictions, then we are not exhibiting meekness! We may end up looking good or strong on the surface, but the victory of that is shallow in comparison to the victory obtained through walking meekly by faith.

- Amy Carmichael, a missionary to India, was a great example of what a life characterized by meekness looks like. Through her humble obedience to God's will—and not her own—she left a legacy that truly glorifies God. Although the things she did weren't necessarily logical from a human perspective, Amy continued to step forward in faith and trusted God to shape His plans for her.

- There is no meekness without surrender. If we are determined to hold on to our will, our pride, our plans, our comfort, etc., then we are not in a posture of meek surrender. To become meek, we must submit ourselves to the Highest Authority and put any power we have under His control.

"Blessed are the meek," Jesus said. Therefore, it must be true! "For they will inherit the earth." I found it interesting when, in searching the Bible, unrelated to this study, I came upon Psalm 37:11. "But the meek will inherit the land and enjoy peace and prosperity."

But why do the meek inherit the earth? What does that even mean? Do we get the inheritance now or later???

Imagine, if you will, the finest chocolate shop in Switzerland. The owner has two sons: one who has been learning and following the father's ways of running the shop, and the other who often does whatever he wants without regard to the father's instruction. The first one learns how to mix the ingredients with just the right finesse; he painstakingly learns how to temper the chocolate at the precise temperature; he lovingly prepares the chocolate displays so that others appreciate the quality of the product. The other son, when he even shows up to work, tries to force his agenda on the shop. He pays little attention to the time-tested family recipes but somewhat haphazardly throws things together, expecting them to work. He gets quickly frustrated with the results of his efforts but still refuses to submit to the wise instructions of his father.

I think it is pretty apparent which son should inherit the family business!

When we are meek, we are submitting to the will of God. We are humble and are allowing ourselves to be refined. When we are meek, we show God that we respect His authority, and His desires have become our own. When we become meek, we become someone who God can trust with His creation.

To think and pray about this week:

1. What has stood out to you, or convicted you, the most about meekness? How will you use that insight moving forward?

2. Read Psalm 37. It only says "meek" once, but many of the verses describe meek characteristics. Is there anything in this passage that grabs your attention?

Dear Lord, thank you for these lessons. Thank you for the incredible way you tie different pieces of our lives together for us to see things from a new perspective. Thank you for allowing Jesus to show us what it means to be meek. Just as He submitted to your perfect will, please help us to desire that same humility. Thank you for your patience with us as we try! We love you, Lord. In Jesus' Name, Amen!

Sections 21 – 26

Hunger & Thirst for Righteousness

21

Hunger & Thirst: Definition

*"Blessed are those who hunger and thirst for righteousness, for they will be filled." -**Matthew 5:6***

This is the verse that inspired this entire Beatitudes study. The one that I was puzzling over when I felt the conviction to look at all of the Beatitudes to see how they build upon one another. But this one is a deceptively complex beatitude to study! We have two notable parts of this Beatitude to define: "hunger and thirst" and "righteousness."

Hunger and thirst: Jesus could have replaced that idea with "want," "desire," "seek," "try to be," etc. Instead, He uses the phrase "hunger and thirst" to emphasize a kind of survival instinct. As humans, hunger and thirst remind us to supply our bodies with fuel to stay alive. What we decide to consume, however, makes a big difference in the state of our ultimate health.

Righteousness: Righteousness is defined as "the quality of being morally right." Biblical righteousness is based on the rightness of God. He sets the moral standard for us to pursue. Isaiah 33:22 says, "For the Lord is our judge, the Lord is our lawgiver, the Lord is our king; it is he who will save us." Psalm 11:7 says, "For the Lord is righteous, he loves justice; the upright will see his face."

So, hungering and thirsting after righteousness ultimately means we are trying to live according to God's standard. We are making decisions based on what God says is right, and our actions are in accordance with scriptural principles. We are pursuing holiness.

Righteousness sounds intimidating! That's a lot of pressure—trying to follow Christ's example. And the worst part is that we already know we will never fully succeed! It can be tempting to not even try because we feel defeated before we begin. However…

Jesus didn't say, "Blessed are the righteous"! To discover the blessing of this Beatitude, we do not have to be perfect. We just have to be *pursuing* righteousness, *craving* righteousness, *desiring* righteousness, and not actually *achieving* righteousness. That achievement is reserved for God alone.

Through our habits, we teach our bodies to crave certain foods or drinks. Have you ever had a specific junk food habit, kicked it, and then tried that food months or years later? It usually doesn't satisfy like it once did. The idea of the food may sound good, but once I consume it, it falls short of the memory. The food itself may not have changed—but my tastes have!

Similarly, when we become Christians, we begin to realize that the world's junk never actually fills us up. When we allow our spirits to hunger and thirst after things that are not righteous, we remain unsatisfied. The craving is never met. The itch is never scratched. If we continue pursuing ungodly things, then we are never filled.

Jesus understood that if we try to feed our God-given soul with worldly food—we will remain spiritually hungry, and our growth will be stunted. We must train ourselves to begin craving what we need to be spiritually full and strong. One scriptural morsel at a time. One righteous decision at a time. One Christ-like action at a time. After a while, it will become more and more natural to hunger and thirst after what God says is right, and all that is self-centered and worldly will look less and less appetizing.

To think and pray about:

1. What other scripture verses come to mind about righteousness? How do those shape your interpretation of what it means to be righteous?

2. What are you craving these days? And, therefore, what are you pursuing and consuming?

3. Most of us have conquered the basics of doing what is right. For example, we aren't going to walk into a store and shoplift. However, the more spiritually mature we become, the more we realize the complexity of these "simple" principles and commandments. Ask God to reveal to you or strengthen an existing conviction on an area of your life where you aren't as righteous as you should be.

Dear Lord, thank you for your example of righteousness. Thank you for giving us a standard and instructions to live by. It is sometimes difficult to interpret how your laws apply to our specific situations. However, when we quiet our spirits enough to listen, you will faithfully guide us on the path of righteousness. Please help us to discover ways to strengthen our hunger and thirst for that righteousness. In Jesus' Name, Amen!

22

Hunger & Thirst: Biblical Example

*"Blessed are those who hunger and thirst for righteousness, for they will be filled." -**Matthew 5:6***

*"In the land of Uz, there lived a man whose name was Job. This man was blameless and upright; he feared God and shunned evil." -**Job 1:1***

The story of Job is well-known: a godly man who lived a blessed life, but God allowed him to suffer significant losses—knowing that Job would remain faithful. Job is brought very low; he is angry and frustrated by his new situation. He doesn't understand why God is allowing his life to be completely torn apart. In his anguish, he says,

*"My feet have closely followed his [God's] steps; I have kept to his way without turning aside. I have not departed from the commands of his lips; I have treasured the words of his mouth more than my daily bread. But he stands alone, and who can oppose him? He does whatever he pleases. He carries out his decree against me and many such plans he still has in store. That is why I am terrified before him; when I think of all this, I fear him. God has made my heart faint; the Almighty has terrified me. Yet I am not silenced by the darkness, by the thick darkness that covers my face." -**Job 23:11-17***

Job is clearly hurting. He mentions how he has lived a faithful and righteous life, and he declares how powerful God is. But never once does Job curse, God, even though he complains about his situation. A few chapters later, Job says,

"As surely as God lives, who has denied me justice, the Almighty, who has made my life bitter, as long as I have life within me, the breath of God in my nostrils, my lips will not say anything wicked, and my tongue will not utter lies."
*-**Job 27:2-4***

Job still chooses righteousness, despite his life falling apart. In the first part of his life, he lived righteously, and he reaped many blessings. He hungered for God, and he was satisfied both spiritually and in the flesh. But then, even after the calamities, Job honors God for the sake of honoring God, not in expectation of reciprocity.

He hungered for righteousness, not reward. He thirsted for righteousness, not results. The remarkable testimony in this story is Job faithfully choosing a righteous response, regardless of the outcome. That is the wisdom Jesus shares with us when He says, "Blessed are those who hunger and thirst after righteousness." If we are so in awe and enamored with our Creator that we want to follow Him no matter what, then we begin to crave obedience to Him more than we crave anything else. We begin to realize that this righteousness brings us closer to God because our focus is on pleasing Him and not ourselves.

It is easy to live by God's standards when those standards are favorable to us. It is easy to be generous when we have much, it is easy to be loving when we feel loved, and it is easy to walk in faithful obedience when we experience positive results. However, like Job, we are called to live righteously even when it appears the Lord's favor is being withheld; and even when we do the right thing and it doesn't make us feel good, or the results are not what we hoped they would be.

Our soul is nourished and filled, not through our situation, but by our obedience to God's calling and our faith in His character. If we are hungry and thirsty for righteousness, then when we obey, our soul will be satisfied even if our flesh is uncomfortable.

To think and pray about:

1. Have you ever read through Job? Does anything else stand out to you about his righteous behavior?

2. Isaiah 51 begins like this: "Listen to me, you who pursue righteousness and who seek the Lord: Look to the rock from which you were cut and to the quarry from which you were hewn." Read Isaiah 51: 1-16. Three times it mentions "righteousness" and "salvation" in the same sentence. How do you think these two concepts are related?

3. Are there any other Bible stories or characters that come to mind who "hungered and thirsted for righteousness"? Perhaps Paul, David, Joshua, Noah, or someone else! What can you learn from their examples?

Dear Lord, thank you for the story of Job. Thank you especially for the ending of the story, which shows you restoring blessing to his life. Although things were dark for him while he suffered, you never abandoned him, and he never cursed you. Let us also learn to honor you in our dark times. Help us learn to crave obedience itself and not the reward of obedience. We love you, Lord. In Jesus' Name, Amen!

23

Hunger & Thirst: Stumbling Blocks

"Blessed are those who hunger and thirst for righteousness, for they will be filled." -**Matthew 5:6**

As I began to think about what prevents me from being hungry and thirsty for righteousness, my first thought was the obvious: I'm hungry for other things! I'm hungry for validation, encouragement, peace, joy, personal fulfillment, spiritual fruit, etc. While I think this is a very valid stumbling block, and we must often retrain our hunger pangs to reflect what is truly missing in our life (more Jesus), there is another stumbling block that is perhaps even more serious:

When we stop being hungry.

What about those seasons or moments when we are so "blah," discouraged, tired, angry, bitter, sad, etc., that we aren't even feeling hungry for anything? We sit there and mindlessly consume whatever crosses our path, not caring if it benefits us or not. Like someone sitting on the sofa devouring an entire bag of potato chips, we aren't even hungry for what is in front of us, yet we still keep munching away! It doesn't satisfy us, and it prevents us from being hungry for what would benefit us.

Scrolling through social media, aimlessly playing games on the phone, partaking in gossip, harboring anxious or bitter thoughts, being caught in sinful patterns, and pursuing anything that is not of God: these are things that cause us to lose our hunger. They are distractions and can make us numb to any hunger pangs we should be experiencing.

But how do we become hungry and thirsty for righteousness? Start consuming it! Break away from the things that are blocking our hunger—even for just 5 minutes—and make a conscious effort to seek God. Then maybe another time you can break away for 10 minutes, or even 30 minutes.

When you find yourself in a time of mindless consumption, decide to read a Bible verse, sing a worship song, pray, encourage a friend, take a step of obedience you've been avoiding, etc.

Some of us have already experienced hunger and thirst for righteousness—but not 24 hours each day. I am quite motivated in the early part of the day, pursuing righteousness and communing with the Lord. But then those evening hours begin to sneak up, and I compromise more and more—choosing things of no value to occupy my time and remaining energy. Or maybe, I'm pretty good at keeping focused on God, except when around certain people or situations.

We may not naturally crave vegetables, but we can all agree that they are beneficial to our health. Yet, the more that we eat them, the more accustomed to the taste we become. As we eat more vegetables and less sugar/junk food, our body begins to develop a hunger for them. The more we get into that habit, the more the hunger will intensify, and the less appealing all that previous junk becomes. I've even gone back and tasted something I used to enjoy, like Dr. Pepper, and found it to taste pretty awful.

We may not naturally crave righteousness. In fact, our flesh is at constant odds against us craving it. However, the more we pursue it, the hungrier we get for it. The more time we spend in God's presence, the more we desire it. The more we worship, the more we find things worth worshipping God for. The more we obey, the more we find joy in obedience. The more we read the scriptures, the more alive and appealing they become.

But we won't hunger and thirst for something that we've never consumed. Instead, we will just continue to consume random things to fill the void. Psalm 34:8 says, "Taste and see that the Lord is good." The next time you find yourself in a time where your hunger is blocked by all that you are mindlessly consuming, take an intentional bite of something righteous. You just may find your hunger awaken.

To think and pray about:

1. Read the rest of Psalm 34, verses 8-22. Do the promises given to the righteous whet your appetite for righteousness? What else motivates you towards righteousness?

2. What other stumbling blocks have you experienced that block your hunger for righteousness? What practical steps can you take this week to awaken or reawaken that hunger?

3. Do you find that your hunger for righteousness comes and goes? Ask God to help show you the patterns or situations where you crave things other than Him.

Dear Lord, thank you for this day. Thank you for giving us amazing bodies that will crave the nutrients we are lacking. Thank you for helping us see parallels between the physical and spiritual worlds so that we can better understand them. Please help us to recognize the areas in our lives where we are not as hungry or thirsty for righteousness as we should be. Please show us individually the steps toward righteousness you would have us take. Give us the courage and strength to follow those convictions. We love you, Lord. In Jesus' Name, Amen!

24

Hunger & Thirst: Modern Example

*"Blessed are those who hunger and thirst for righteousness, for they will be filled." -**Matthew 5:6***

When someone is doing good in the name of God, it can be difficult to discern their motives, and therefore what they are hungry for. Are they seeking validation and reward, or are they truly just walking in obedience for the love of God? Since we cannot peer into someone's heart, we must find our righteousness-thirsting role models differently: looking at the second half of what Jesus said: "for they will be filled."

If someone is driven by their desire to do what is right for the sake of righteousness, then they will be satisfied by their obedience and not the outcome. If someone is hungry for righteousness because they love the righteous Creator, then they will be filled, and there will be no void in their life. If someone is thirsty for Jesus, they will be content. They may go through seasons of drought, but they won't despair. There may be emptiness all around them, but they will remain filled. Their efforts may appear fruitless, but they will be content.

But while people might become famous during the fruitful seasons of their pursuit of righteousness, they don't become famous for their *hunger* for righteousness. In fact, because they aren't focused on people-pleasing, they may fall out of favor entirely while still retaining their hunger for righteousness. So, choosing a role model based on a successful ministry doesn't necessarily mean that person is the right role model for this particular verse.

However, someone comes to mind—someone who lived a humble life and whose legacy does, reflect his hunger and thirst for righteousness: Brother Lawrence. For those who haven't heard of him before, Brother Lawrence was a monk in the 1600s who is remembered for his close relationship with God. A series of letters that he wrote towards the end of his life was later published into a book called <u>The Practice of the Presence of God</u>. Here are some excerpts of his writings, which give some insight into how one who is hungry and thirsty for righteousness might approach their life:

> *"The account I can give you is this: Having found in many books different methods of going to God and diverse practices of the spiritual life, I thought this would serve rather to puzzle me than facilitate what I sought after, which was nothing but how to become wholly God's. This made me resolve to give the all for the All. After having given myself wholly to God, to make all the satisfaction I could for my sins, I renounced, for the love of Him, everything that was not He, and I began to live as if there was none but He and I in the world.*
>
> *Sometimes I considered myself before Him as a poor criminal at the feet of his judge. At other times I beheld Him in my heart as my Father, as my God. I worshipped Him the oftenest I could, keeping my mind in His holy presence and recalling it as often as I found it wandered from Him. I made this my business, not only at the appointed times of prayer but all the time; every hour, every minute, even in the height of my work, I drove from my mind everything that interrupted my thoughts of God."*

He continues further along in the letter:

> *"When we are faithful to keep ourselves in His holy presence, and set Him always before us, this hinders our offending Him, and doing anything that may displease Him. It also begets in us a holy freedom, and, if I may so speak, a familiarity with God, where, when we ask, He supplies the graces we need. Over time, by often repeating these acts, they become habitual, and the presence of God becomes quite natural to us.*
>
> *Please give Him thanks with me, for His great goodness towards me, which I can never sufficiently express, and for the many favors He has done to so miserable a sinner as I am. May all things praise Him. Amen."*

And here is where we really see the blessing of being filled when righteousness is what we seek:

> *"God has many ways of drawing us to Himself. He sometimes seems to hide Himself from us. But faith alone ought to be our support. Faith is the foundation of our confidence. We must put all our faith in God. He will not fail us in time of need. I do not know how God will dispose of me but I am always happy. All the*

world suffers and I, who deserve the severest discipline, feel joys so continual and great that I can scarcely contain them."

Brother Lawrence desired to be in God's presence more than anything else in the world. And he lived it out! He did not live a life of luxury—even for a monk. He was born poor, he served in the army and saw many horrors, he considered himself awkward and clumsy, and he became lame. And yet, he experienced such profound peace and contentment in his lowly state that he gained a reputation for his pursuit of God and rejection of everything that distracted from it.

To think and pray about:

1. What stands out to you from the Brother Lawrence quotes? Is there any tidbit of wisdom that you can apply to your own life right now?

2. While a man or woman may not become famous for hunger and thirsting for righteousness, the closest people might recognize it. Is there anyone that you have known who has faithfully exhibited this? If they are still in your life, consider reaching out and asking them to share some wisdom on how they have stayed hungry for God instead of other things.

3. Paul says, in Philippians 4: 11-13, "I am not saying this because I am in need, for I have learned to be content whatever the circumstances. I know what it is to be in need, and I know what it is to have plenty. I have learned the secret of being content in any and every situation, whether well fed or hungry, whether living in plenty or in want. I can do all this through him who gives me strength." Based on what we know about Paul's life, it would seem that his contentment stemmed from his thirst for righteousness. Paul focused on his relationship with Christ, and therefore found the strength to be content. Are you content in every situation?

Dear Lord, thank you for this day. Thank you for continued opportunities to seek your presence and find our contentment in you. Thank you for the wisdom of Brother Lawrence and that his legacy has lasted this long. Please help us to use it as a reminder for ourselves that you are faithful to satisfy us when we hunger after your righteousness. Let us learn the discipline to reject other cravings and instead recognize that any emptiness we feel should be filled by you and nothing else. We love you, Lord. In Jesus' Name, Amen!

25

Hunger & Thirst: Challenge

"Blessed are those who hunger and thirst for righteousness, for they will be filled." -**Matthew 5:6**

I don't know about you, but I get cravings sometimes. Sometimes they are healthy cravings, and sometimes they are not so healthy. Over the years, however, I've learned to train myself to use my cravings to identify my deficiencies. If I'm craving a lot of sugar, usually it's because I'm behind in sleep. If I have a strong hankering for a steak, my iron levels might be low. While consuming what I crave might help meet my true need, that isn't always the case. Eating a bunch of sugar might give me a rush, but it certainly won't help my daily energy issues. Eating a steak might give me some iron, but I need to make sure I'm eating a balanced diet with iron from multiple sources.

There are also cravings I have that are primarily based on habit or routine. I crave an iced caramel latte from Starbucks when I drive to the chiropractor on Friday mornings because I have gone through that drive-through so many times right before I get onto the highway. I crave some time to just mindlessly browse the internet on my phone after I get my youngest son to bed because that time of the day finally feels like "mine." After I do something for God, I crave validation because it feels like proof that I did the right thing. I don't *need* an iced latte, just as I don't *need* a compliment, but they taste good in the moment. If I'm not careful, these habitual cravings might get me stuck into a pattern of pseudo-dependency to where I don't want to move forward unless they are fulfilled.

Getting stuck in these craving cycles can be annoying and unhealthy. We aren't truly getting nourished, and we aren't truly growing to our full potential. Some cravings are more harmless than others, but when we depend on anything other than God's grace to get through our days, then those cravings have the potential to become stumbling blocks and idols. We aren't always called to give everything up, but we must be willing.

This week, take time to identify something you crave that you are convicted of fulfilling with righteousness instead. That could look like when you crave validation, you remind yourself to stand firm on your identity in Christ. Or maybe you take a break from a literal food or drink item you crave, and when the craving hits, you remember to feed on God's Word instead. When you crave the comfort of a fruitless habit, perhaps you replace it with something that serves someone else.

Just pick one thing to focus on—one small aspect of life to surrender and establish a deeper connection to Jesus. Address what deficiency you are instinctively trying to reverse or what habitual rut you have dug for yourself by pursuing righteousness instead.

To think and pray about:

1. What is the craving in your life that you are convicted to redirect? As you go through the week, take note of your heart and soul's reactions to replacing what you thought you were hungry for with something righteous instead.

2. Find a practical way to address your craving so that when it hits, you already have a plan: a hymn to sing, scripture to lean on, action to take, etc. Use this not only as a tool for yourself but also as a weapon against the temptations you are presented with.

3. Read through Proverbs 21. Do any verses stand out to you?

Dear Lord, thank you for providing all we need, even when at times we think we need more. Lord, please help us to identify our deficiencies and our dependencies. Give us the wisdom to choose something else that is of your design instead. Let us gain more insight into how you are working in our lives through this challenge, and may we grow closer to you in the process. Please fill the gaps in our lives with your righteousness. We love you, Lord. In Jesus' Name, Amen!

26

Hunger & Thirst: Conclusion

*"Blessed are those who hunger and thirst for righteousness, for they will be filled." -**Matthew 5:6***

To be hungry and thirsty for righteousness is ultimately to be desiring rightness with God, to be in a relationship with Him. To be connected to Him. And Jesus promises that we will be blessed and filled!

Here is a summary of what we have reflected on during this Beatitude:

- Righteousness is defined as "the quality of being morally right." As Christians, we believe God sets the standard of what is right. He is the only one truly righteous, but we should seek to do our best to follow his instructions.

- Job was a man who sought to be righteous. The Enemy accused him of only being righteous because of the blessings he was receiving. However, when God allowed those blessings to be taken away, Job continued to honor God even though there was no reward. Job knew that it was important to be righteous, for the sake of righteousness, not for reward.

- Hungering and thirsting for things that are not God prevents us from hungering for God Himself. But not only that, mindlessly consuming junk to the point where we aren't hungry for anything is also a problem. When we are continually grazing on whatever is put in front of us, we miss out on the opportunity to truly hunger for God and His righteousness. When we can tear ourselves away and consciously seek God, we can reestablish the hunger for Him that had been deadened.

- Brother Lawrence, a French monk, was a man who developed a hunger and thirst for righteousness, and he maintained that hunger by striving to always remain in God's presence. Brother Lawrence understood the importance of relationship and communion with God and that staying in God's presence helped him deal with life's trials righteously.

- Our cravings can reveal our deficiencies and distractions. If we can learn to redirect our cravings, then we can begin to look to God to satisfy us.

Hunger and thirst are basic human instincts. They indicate our natural leanings towards self-preservation and sustenance. Without hunger and thirst, we may forget to consume. However, just like pain, which is another basic function that helps us, hunger and thirst can sometimes be a little irritating. I don't want to feel hungry and thirsty sometimes—I just want to keep moving forward with the other things I've set out to do. I don't want to have those hunger pangs reminding me to eat or a dry and scratchy throat to make me pick up a drink.

But herein lies the blessing of hungering and thirsting for righteousness: being filled. We are filled because of our relationship with God. Jesus says, in John 15:5, "I am the vine; you are the branches. If you remain in me and I in you, you will bear much fruit; apart from me, you can do nothing." Our hunger for righteousness should ultimately lead us to a relationship with Jesus. And if we remain in Him, He is in us, and we are filled. Not in a stagnant way, but in a life-giving, xylem-flowing kind of way.

When we are connected to Jesus, we are filled and satisfied. We become less concerned with pursuing the things of this world, and we are content with righteousness as our reward.

To think and pray about:

1. What has stood out or convicted you the most about this Beatitude? Have you identified any deficiencies, fruitless habits, or cravings that you need to address? Be sure to keep these in prayer as you seek to pursue righteousness first and foremost.

2. How can you remind yourself, on a practical level, to stay hungry and thirsty for righteousness? Is there a particular Bible verse that helps to bring you back to it?

3. Matthew 6:33 tells us, "But seek ye first the kingdom of God, and his righteousness; and all these things shall be added unto you." (KJV). This verse follows a similar pattern to Matthew 5:6. Seek first (hunger and thirst), righteousness, all these things shall be added unto you (you will be filled). Are there any other verses you know of that provide a similar promise to the pursuit of righteousness?

Dear Lord, thank you for this day. Thank you for desiring a relationship with us, and thank you for filling us when we seek you. Lord, please help us to each understand what righteousness is and how to hunger for it. Let us focus more on doing what is right because we love you, not because we seek reward. Lord, please help us to be satisfied as we remain connected to you: our source of everything good. We love you, Lord. In Jesus' Name, Amen!

Sections 27 – 32

Merciful

27

Merciful: Definition

*"Blessed are the merciful, for they will be shown mercy." –**Matthew 5:7***

To understand the word "merciful," we have to first look at the definition of "mercy." The Greek word for "mercy" is "Eleos," which means "mercy, pity, compassion." Oxford Dictionary defines "mercy" as "compassion or forgiveness shown toward someone whom it is within one's power to punish or harm."

So, "merciful" essentially means "showing or exercising mercy."

When I first think of the words "mercy" and "merciful," I think of a courtroom where the judge has compassion on the defendant and gives them a less harsh sentence than deserved. I also think of two men dueling with swords, and one gets pinned to the ground by the other, sword tip to the neck. But then the man with the advantage releases his opponent—showing mercy by not harming when he could.

Mercy is a very powerful part of our Christian faith. Without mercy, there would be no Christianity. It is because of God's mercy that He sent Jesus in the first place! He shows compassion and forgiveness to humanity—which is within His power to punish or harm.

But why do we even need mercy? Romans 3:23 reminds us that "for all have sinned and fall short of the glory of God." And Romans 5:8 says, "But God demonstrates his love for us in this: While we were still sinners, Christ died for us." Sin created the separation between God and us and put us into the category of deserving punishment. However, because God is merciful, He created a way for forgiveness.

Jesus says, "Blessed are the merciful," which tells us that just as God has had mercy on us, we should extend mercy to others. It is a way to honor God and show Him that we accept and appreciate the mercy He has given us.

Showing mercy doesn't just mean forgiving people when they do horrible things to us. We have the opportunity to show mercy for minor insults, forgetful errors, and inconveniences they cause us. We also have the opportunity to show mercy to anyone who needs our help—whether we feel they deserve it or not. Mercy is about our heart's decision to show compassion and has nothing to do with the other person. Obviously, we may be more inclined to show mercy to someone who is remorseful or grateful, but Jesus doesn't say, "Blessed are the ones who extend mercy sometimes"! We should strive to show mercy at every opportunity we can muster the strength to. The more we practice this Godly habit of showing merciful forgiveness and compassion, the easier it can become.

It is also worth noting, however, that mercy is not a weakness. It is not about allowing people to take advantage or cause you harm. It also isn't giving people whatever they want, with no regard to our own needs. We can be both merciful and cautious. We condemn the sin, don't enable the sin while loving the person who has sinned. Mercy offers protection for our hearts because it saves us from bitterness.

To think and pray about:

1. What scene comes to mind when you think of mercy and merciful? How does that shape your approach to extending it to others?

2. Have you ever forgiven someone who has wronged you? Have you shown mercy and compassion? Why do you think these protect our hearts from bitterness instead of making us more vulnerable?

3. Psalm 51 begins with, "Have mercy on me, O God, according to your unfailing love; according to your great compassion blot out my transgressions." Read Psalm 51 in its entirety and make a note of what stands out to you about God's mercy for us.

Dear Lord, thank you for your mercy. Thank you for giving us the example of extending mercy even when we don't deserve it. Thank you for your kindness and compassion, and patience, even as we neglect your words over and over again. Please help us to see how we can be more merciful to those around us. Show us opportunities to be a light in those dark situations, that through the extension of mercy, your love would be felt. We love you, Lord. In Jesus' Name, Amen!

28

Merciful: Biblical Example

*"Blessed are the merciful, for they will be shown mercy." –**Matthew 5:7***

Mercy isn't only about forgiveness, as our definition shows us. Mercy, remember, is also about compassion and pity—even when it is in one's power or right to refuse those mercies. A great example of this is found in the book of Ruth.

Ruth's husband, brother-in-law, and father-in-law were all dead. Her mother in law, Naomi, planned to go back to Bethlehem, so she told Ruth and the other daughter-in-law to go back to their own families:

> *"But Ruth replied, "Don't urge me to leave you or to turn back from you. Where you go, I will go, and where you stay, I will stay. Your people will be my people and your God my God. Where you die, I will die, and there I will be buried. May the Lord deal with me, be it ever so severely, if even death separates you and me." When Naomi realized that Ruth was determined to go with her, she stopped urging her."*
> *–**Ruth 1:16-18***

Ruth had every right to leave Naomi. She had the legal right, as her husband was dead, and she had the social right because Naomi specifically released her from any obligations. However, Ruth chose to have pity and compassion on Naomi and accompany her. Ruth chose to be merciful. Through her story, we also get a glimpse of how God uses Ruth's mercy to show His mercy and compassion for both Naomi and Ruth. Ruth even ends up being blessed in a very tangible way: giving birth to a son who would end up in the family line of Jesus!

What is so interesting about this story of mercy is that it shows us mercy is a choice. Ruth wouldn't have sinned if she left Naomi! No one would have blamed her or made her feel bad about it. Leaving Naomi would have been perfectly justified. However, being merciful is about surrendering our right to something for the good of someone else. We don't have to do it. We are usually under no obligation to show mercy, compassion, or pity. However, Jesus makes it a point to teach us that the merciful are blessed and will be shown mercy.

Through Ruth's example, we see that her choice of mercy was a wise one. However, that is only in hindsight. Often, when we are at the crossroads between exercising our right or extending mercy, we do not know how it will play out. It can be challenging to find the courage to move forward with mercy because we fear being hurt or taken advantage of. Ultimately, however, we can only control our actions and not those of someone else.

When we choose mercy, we do choose an unknown outcome. However, in addition to that unknown, we are allowing God to work for our good and the good of others. Ruth could have gone back to her family—that was the safe option, relatively predictable, and within her right. However, because she chose mercy, even though it was initially more difficult, Ruth put herself in a position where God could incorporate her into a story so much bigger than herself.

Each time we choose mercy, we show God our willingness to be used by Him. We show Him that we are willing to lay down our rights, or perceived rights, to comfort reparations and control. Even our small gestures of pity, compassion, and mercy can be incorporated into a larger purpose—the blessings paling in comparison to what we are giving up.

To think and pray about:

1. Have you made a choice for mercy recently? Perhaps inconveniencing yourself out of compassion for another, canceling a debt someone owed you, or taking pity on someone that you were not obligated to serve? What made you choose mercy?

2. In Matthew 18:21-35, Jesus tells the parable of the unmerciful servant. Read this passage. What further meaning does it give you to Jesus saying, "Blessed are the merciful for they will receive mercy"?

3. Can you think of an opportunity you have had to show mercy but chose not to? Ask God to grant you insight into the situation so that you may be better prepared the next time an opportunity for mercy arises.

Amy M. Blindt

Dear Lord, thank you for this day. Thank you that your mercies are new each morning—that you continually make a choice to show us mercy. Thank you also for the story of Ruth and the lessons we can glean from it. Thank you for giving her the boldness and courage to choose a merciful but unknown future instead of a safe and predictable one. Lord, please show us ways that we can do the same. We love you, Lord. In Jesus' Name, Amen!

29

Merciful: Stumbling Blocks

"Blessed are the merciful, for they will be shown mercy." —**Matthew 5:7**

Mercy, as you can see, begins with "ME." To fully understand mercy, we have to start with identifying what belongs to ME. What is rightfully MinE? What is owed to ME? So, for example:

- This money belongs to ME, and I have a right to keep it for myself
- My time is MinE, and I have a right to do whatever I want with it
- That debt is owed to ME, and I have a right to claim it
- This comfort zone is MinE, and since you violated it, I have a right to be angry

The first part of mercy is about "me"!

But that's where people often get stuck and forget to complete the steps of mercy. Once we have identified a threat to, or violation of, what is ours, we are focused on ourselves. And tearing that focus away from ourselves often proves difficult. We find comfort in looking at what belongs to us. There is security in the certainty that we are in the right (or at least we think we are!). But staying at "ME" never leads to "MErcy."

If we want to get into the practice of being merciful, we must learn to complete the act of mercy! After we identify what belongs to "ME," then we must remember to tell ourselves, "Relinquish Control of what's Yours!"

"Relinquish" is a reminder of our choice—because mercy is a choice. When we relinquish something, we give up our claim to it. We surrender what is rightfully ours for the benefit of another. Whether mercy is taking the form of debt cancellation, compassionate giving, or mercifully serving, it involves us giving up something that belongs to "ME."

"Control" is a reminder that when we relinquish something, we no longer dictate what happens to it. We can extend mercy in its various forms, but we cannot control how it is received. That being said, we must be content with our obedience in showing mercy—not relying on the responses of others to tell us we did the right thing. How others respond to our merciful acts is outside of our control.

"Of what's Yours" is a reminder that to become merciful, we must be willing to step outside of ourselves, look ourselves in the eye, and say, "Relinquish Control of what's Yours." Mercy won't happen if we stay wrapped up in our own agenda and emotions.It requires us to leave the "me" behind for a greater purpose.

Those earlier sentences, when completed with a merciful heart, might look like this:

- This money belongs to ME, and I have a right to keep it for myself, but I choose to compassionately spend some on another person.
- My time is MinE, and I have a right to do whatever I want with it, but I will choose to serve others with it.
- That debt is owed to ME, and I have a right to claim it, but I choose to forgive the debt instead.
- This comfort zone is MinE, and since you violated it, I have a right to be angry; however, I will choose to look at the situation from your perspective as well.

Mercy, while beginning with "me," must end with the focus away from "me." Don't get stuck dwelling on what is yours or what you lay claim to. To get into a habit of mercy and become a merciful person, you must get into the habit of recognizing what is yours and then surrendering it. Remember, recognize what belongs to "ME," but then Relinquish Control of what's Yours!

To think and pray about:

1. Do you notice a repeating situation in your life where you struggle to offer mercy even though you are convicted to? What can this teach you about yourself and your priorities?

2. Sometimes, it is easier to extend mercy when we remember the mercies we received when undeserved. Read Daniel 9:4-19. It is a powerful prayer outlining the sin of the people and asking for God's mercy. We would do well to be so contrite!

3. What is the most challenging part of mercy for you to understand or apply? Or do you feel that you are already characterized as being a merciful person?

Dear Lord, thank you for mercy. Thank you for giving us what we do not deserve and showing compassion to us. Lord, please help us to get into better habits of showing mercy. Give us the opportunities to have our acts of mercy be reflections of Your love and grace— that others may know you better. We love you, Lord. In Jesus' Name, Amen!

30

Merciful: Modern Example

*"Blessed are the merciful, for they will be shown mercy." –**Matthew 5:7***

Mercy is such a beautiful thing when modeled humbly! Because it frequently has an external component, when someone chooses to extend mercy, we get to see the choice!

One such example of merciful forgiveness and compassion is found in the story of Elisabeth Elliott. She was initially made famous for being a missionary's wife who was brutally murdered by a savage tribe in Ecuador. Her husband, Jim, was one of 5 men who were speared to death as they tried to make contact and bring Jesus to this isolated group, known as the Auca Indians. This happened in 1956 and made headlines worldwide.

Despite such a tragedy, Elisabeth was firm in her conviction to be a missionary in Ecuador. She remained there with her infant daughter and helped some of the friendlier natives that had already embraced the missionaries. However, no one would have blamed her for returning to America and leaving Ecuador behind. For many, that would have been the logical thing for her to do. However, when the opportunity came for Elisabeth to make contact with that same group who killed her husband, she immediately did so.

The mercy and compassion that she showed for people who were so outwardly unlovable are astounding! Not only did she choose not to harbor bitterness over the murder, but she sought to serve those people and show Christ's love to them! To better understand how one person could exude such mercy, let us take a look at some of Elisabeth's writings:

> (Before the murders) *"The other wives and I talked together one night about the possibility of becoming widows. What would we do? God gave us peace of heart, and confidence that whatever might happen, His Word would hold. We knew that*

> *'when He Putteth forth His sheep, He goeth before them.'* God's leading was unmistakable up to this point. Each of us knew when we married our husbands that there would never be any question about who came first—God and His work held first place in each life. It was the condition of true discipleship; it became devastatingly meaningful now." --taken from <u>Through Gates of Splendor,</u> by Elisabeth Elliot

The first step that Elisabeth took towards mercy happened even before she had reason to show it! By already surrendering her marriage before it was in jeopardy, she could more gracefully transition from wife to widow. Her priorities were already established—God's direction first, everything else second. While that decision did not negate the pain and hardships that ensued, since she had already been prepared to let go, she did so.

> (After the murders, wondering what God's plan was for reaching the Auca people) *"I simply asked the Lord to do what He wanted to do about it. For once in my life I had no suggestions to make to Him about how He was to do it. I placed myself in His hands, saying that if He wanted to give me a part in reaching the Aucas, I was ready. I had noticed throughout the Bible that, when God asked a man to do something, methods, means, materials, and specific directions were always provided. The man had one thing to do: obey. This would have to be the only thing that mattered with regard to the Aucas."* –taken from <u>The Savage My Kinsman</u>, by Elisabeth Elliot

The second thing that helped Elisabeth stay focused on mercy was seeking to be obedient to God. Her purpose outweighed her pain, and she was ready to be a part of serving the Aucas—if it was what God wanted of her. She wasn't trying to force herself into the situation; she was just available and listening should the call come. We know, looking back, that the call *did* come, and Elisabeth was highly instrumental in bringing Christianity to a people that the rest of the world ignored.

Elisabeth Elliot's testimony has inspired countless other Christians throughout the world. After Jim was murdered, she could have gone back to the United States and lived a quiet and humble life. However, because she was merciful and compassionate, even to those who did not deserve it from her, the legacy she left behind is incredibly powerful.

We would all do well to remember that choosing mercy requires us to surrender what we feel entitled to. If we can learn to be in the habit of surrendering daily, then it will be easier for us to become quickly merciful when the occasion arises. However, even after we have lost something and are angry about it, we have the opportunity to surrender. Also, clinging to our purpose instead of our pain, inconvenience, etc., will help us choose mercy. And if we are unsure of what God is calling us to do, we can ask Him for guidance and wisdom—again, taking the focus off ourselves.

To think and pray about:

1. What stands out to you or challenges you from the Elisabeth Elliot quotes?

2. Micah 6:8 says, "He has shown you, O mortal, what is good, and what does the Lord require of you? To act justly and to love mercy and to walk humbly with your God." How does this solidify Elisabeth Elliot's convictions to stay in the mission field even after her husband's death? How does this verse convict you?

3. Elisabeth Elliot had already considered the possibility of losing her husband and had surrendered that scenario to God. Are there some things in your life that you are convicted to surrender as well? Surrendering them does not mean you will lose them, but it may prepare your heart to get into the habit of surrender so that you are more likely to extend mercy when the opportunity arises…

Dear Lord, thank you for the story of Elisabeth Elliot. Thank you for her faithfulness to You and the example that she set in trusting You. Thank you that she had the courage to persevere and show mercy to those who had wronged her. Thank you for her example of surrender to your plans for her life rather than her own. Please show us what we are holding onto too tightly, and help us to become prepared to show mercy and compassion. We love you, Lord. In Jesus' Name, Amen!

31

Merciful: Challenge

*"Blessed are the merciful, for they will be shown mercy." -**Matthew 5:7***

Mercy is a choice we can make. However, Jesus offers further wisdom on the subject when He shares the Parable of the Unmerciful Servant in Matthew 18. In this story, a king was settling debts with his servants. One servant had a great debt, and the king initially wanted to make the servant sell everything he had to pay that debt. The servant's life and livelihood would have essentially been ruined. In despair, the servant begged for mercy, so the king had pity and canceled the great debt.

Then, the servant went and found another servant who owed him a small amount of money. The servant insisted that it be paid back immediately. When the other servant begged for mercy, the unmerciful servant had him thrown into prison. The king caught wind of this and was furious. He threw the unmerciful servant into prison so that he could work to pay off the enormous debt. Jesus ends the parable by saying:

> *"This is how my heavenly Father will treat each of you unless you forgive your brother or sister from your heart." -**Matthew 18:35***

The primary problem that the unmerciful servant had was that he quickly forgot the mercy extended to him. Away from the context of his debt being forgiven, his actions toward the other servant seem justified. There was a debt to be paid, and so measures were taken to guarantee repayment.

However, the key to this parable is in the context. When we see that the unmerciful servant's debt was forgiven, then we are abhorred by his treatment of the other servant. When we know the value of the amount forgiven, then the pettiness of pursuing the smaller debt is highlighted.

We can apply this same concept to our approach to mercy. To inspire our hearts to be merciful, we should remember. We should remember the number of our sins that God has forgiven. We should remember the blessings we have received and the provision we have experienced. We should remember the joyful moments and peaceful moments. We should remember the decisions we have made and the problems we have gracefully avoided. When we remember these things, we can more easily be merciful and compassionate to those we encounter. When we recognize the amount of mercy we have experienced, then we are more likely to choose to be merciful to others.

Forgiveness, compassion, and pity are all forms of mercy—what can you do this week to show it to someone else? If you are struggling, then pray for God to remind you of the mercies you have received. Keep the memories in the forefront of your mind so that you are prepared to offer mercy when the opportunity presents itself.

To think and pray about:

1. Read Matthew 18:21-35. Does anything else stand out to you about this parable?

2. The "golden rule" is taken from the famous verse Matthew 7:12: "So in everything, do to others what you would have them do to you, for this sums up the Law and the Prophets." How can this verse also shape our approach to mercy?

3. Is there an act of mercy you have been withholding lately? Look at the situation in the context of all the mercies you have been given and see if that changes your perspective and heart towards the other person.

Dear Lord, thank you for the wisdom of Jesus and the parables He told. Thank you for the conviction that comes when we look at the context of our own lives and the amount of mercies you have extended to us. Thank you for allowing us to learn these lessons, even imperfectly. Lord, please help open our eyes this week to the mercies you would have us extend to others. Show us how we can be compassionate and forgiving—reflecting your light and compassion. We love you, Lord. In Jesus' Name, Amen!

32

Merciful: Conclusion

*"Blessed are the merciful, for they will be shown mercy." -**Matthew 5:7***

The lesson of mercy is an important one. Although it is a choice we can make, the benefits of making this choice should encourage us towards mercy. Yet, we are much more likely to choose mercy when we remember the mercy that has been shown to us. Because of this cycle, we are also drawn closer to God.

Here is a summary of what we have reflected on during this Beatitude:

- Mercy encompasses forgiveness, pity, and compassion. Because of this, mercy can look many different ways and come in many various opportunities.

- In the Bible, Ruth shows us a great example of mercy, and through her story, we see that mercy is a choice. It wouldn't have been sinful for Ruth to go back to her own people and leave Naomi, but because Ruth showed mercy, her story and impact in the world became much more important.

- One of the major stumbling blocks of mercy is focusing on "me." When we decide to surrender what is rightfully ours for the benefit of another, we allow God to use our story for a greater purpose. After we identify what belongs to "ME," then we should complete the process and tell ourselves to "Relinquish Control of what's Yours!

- Elisabeth Elliot's choice to minister to the same people who murdered her missionary husband reveals how God's purpose for her life outweighed any pain she experienced. Her obedience to this calling is an inspiration for us also to extend compassion, pity, and forgiveness whenever we are called to do so.

- When we feel hard-hearted towards someone and desire to withhold mercy, we need to remember. We should remember our debts that have been forgiven, and we should remember the compassion and pity that we have been shown. Without the context of these memories, we may feel much more justified in being unmerciful. That is the trap that the unmerciful steward found himself in, told by Jesus in Matthew 18.

Jesus says that the blessing of the merciful is that they will be shown mercy. God has extended many mercies to us, and He continues to do so throughout our lifetime. When we show mercy to others, then our heart is put in a position to see the mercy of God. Mercy softens our hearts, and we become more in awe of God's graciousness over our lives. This begins and then sustains a cycle of worshipful mercy—where we are showing mercy to others because of an outpouring of love and gratitude to God.

To think and pray about:

1. What aspect of mercy (forgiveness, compassion, pity) do you feel most convicted towards in this season of life?

2. Lamentations 3:22-23 (KJV) says, "It is of the Lord's mercies that we are not consumed because his compassions fail not. They are new every morning: great is thy faithfulness." How does this image of "mercies are new every morning" make your heart feel towards God?

3. Do you have any lingering questions for God about what forms mercy can take in your own life? Ask Him to give you clear opportunities if they are not already apparent.

Dear Lord, thank you for mercy. Thank you for daily, endless mercies that are even fresher each morning. Thank you for the stories of others who have chosen mercy so that we can be inspired. But most of all, thank you for providing the choice of mercy as a way to draw us closer to you. Thank you for allowing it to soften our hearts and posture us for worship. Please help us to begin and maintain this cycle of gratitude so that the way we treat others is a reflection of how you have treated us. We love you, Lord. In Jesus' Name, Amen!

Sections 33 – 38

Pure in Heart

33

Pure in Heart: Definition

*"Blessed are the pure in heart, for they will see God." –***Matthew 5:8**

In the dictionary, pure means "not mixed or adulterated with any other substance or material," "without any extraneous and unnecessary elements," and "free of any contamination." So, pure water is simply hydrogen and oxygen—no dirt, chlorine, etc. Pure gold is just gold with no impurities or other metals. "Pure" implies that only the intended material is present. "Pure" implies perfection.

From a spiritual standpoint, "pure in heart" sounds very intimidating and unachievable. We are sinful people; how can we possibly be considered "pure"? Even the slightest imperfection causes something to become "impure." However, Jesus knew we would never be sinless—that's why He came to die in the first place! And He didn't say, "Blessed are the *pure*." Instead, He said, "pure *in heart*."

Our heart is what drives us. It is our innermost being. Our heart is where our desires and emotions live, and it is not a perfect place! But if we are pure in our hearts, Jesus says we are blessed.

What does this actually look like? To be pure in heart while worshipping God means that we are doing it solely to honor Him, not because it makes us look good. To be pure in heart while serving means that we are doing it solely out of love with no desire for reward. To be pure in heart while doing anything means that our motive is of God and is not mixed with any additional motives. Our motive must be pure.

Children often have pure motives, which is why they are usually called innocents. However, as we grow and develop, the world has a way of contaminating us. What began as pure is now mixed with other elements. We learn fear, greed, ambition, etc. These impure driving factors get mixed with the God-honoring motives that we are called to.

Fortunately, there are ways to become pure again. Just like water can be filtered and cleaned, and gold can be refined in the fire, God can and will purify our hearts. However, just like for water and gold, purification is a process. For our hearts, God may reveal to us the dirt in the filter He is using to clean us. We may not like what we see, but it is up to us to allow the impurities to remain or let them be filtered out. Or there may be other occasions where we are being refined like gold. God may allow trials and pressures in our lives so that all of the extra stuff in our hearts is burned away. Our true and pure self is then revealed.

Being confronted with our impurities, or being refined through trials, is never comfortable. However, Jesus promises a blessing to those who seek to have a pure heart. We can be thankful that God has not given us an unachievable task or one we must do on our own strength.

> *"If we confess our sins, he is faithful and just and will forgive us our sins and purify us from all unrighteousness." -1 John 1:9*

To think and pray about:

1. What drives you? What REALLY drives you? As you go through the day, take a moment and think about why you are doing specific tasks or saying certain things. Ask God to reveal to you your true motives and to show you if there are some adjustments to be made in your heart.

2. Read Titus 2:11-14. It says that Jesus died to purify us so that we would be zealous of good works. Is there anything in that passage that stands out or convicts you?

3. When you think of "pure in heart," what comes to mind? Is this an easy concept for you to grasp or a more complex one?

Dear Lord, thank you for this day. Thank you for the lessons you are always teaching us and for the convictions. It is not usually comfortable to be confronted with our impurities, but please help us learn to be pleased enough with the results that we willingly go through the process. Help us to see how the motives of our hearts can either honor you or make our sacrifices shallow. We love you, Lord. In Jesus' Name, Amen!

34

Pure in Heart: Biblical Example

*"Blessed are the pure in heart, for they will see God." –**Matthew 5:8***

When I think through the vast list of Bible stories, it is much easier to identify stories where the characters were obviously NOT pure in heart. Perhaps it is because the heart is private and personal, and we cannot see inside one another's. We can have more confidence in recognizing blatant evil than we can in recognizing actions that appear Godly but come from a heart that is not honoring God.

As God reminds Samuel in 1 Samuel 16:7b, "The Lord does not look at the things people look at. People look at the outward appearance, but the Lord looks at the heart." Ultimately, He is the only one who can perfectly judge the purity of someone's heart. However, in the warning that Proverbs 4:23 gives us ("Above all else, guard your heart, for everything you do flows from it."), we see that what we do is a result of the state of our hearts. We can therefore look at what a person does to try to surmise what is in their heart.

There is a character in the Bible who gives us several opportunities to see his purity of heart: Joshua, son of Nun. We see that he is not motivated by fear, peer pressure, popular opinion, or his own greatness. He was purely devoted to doing God's will, and the decisions he made show that.

In Numbers 13, Joshua was one of the twelve men appointed by Moses to explore Canaan. The men came back after 40 days and reported that while the land was "flowing with milk and honey," the people who lived there were mighty. Ten of the twelve men discouraged the Israelites from going into the land because of those powerful people. However, Joshua and Caleb did not allow fear to influence their opinion—they trusted that God would fulfill His promise of giving them the land. In that circumstance, their hearts were pure and full of faith.

After Joshua and Caleb expressed their faith that God would give the Israelites the land, "the whole assembly talked about stoning them" (Numbers 14:10). But, just as they did not allow fear to motivate their opinions, they also didn't allow themselves to be swayed by peer pressure. It is much easier to do the right thing when it follows other people's expectations. However, when we mix that desire to please people with the desire to please God, then our hearts are impure. We may tell ourselves that we are trying to please God, but Jesus says that we cannot serve two masters (Matthew 6:24). Joshua proved that he did not have mixed loyalties—his devotion was pure.

Similarly, in Joshua 7, Joshua discovers that Achan has sinned, and all of Israel is being punished for it. The Lord orders Joshua to deal with Achan and his family severely, and Joshua does so. He does so simply and purely out of obedience. He is not concerned with being a popular leader—just one who is dedicated to God. Also, his motives are not for personal reasons—he is not acting out of personal anger or hatred towards Achan.

During the story of the Fall of Jericho, Joshua displays additional purity of heart. God gives him specific instructions on what the Israelites should do (march around the city for seven days, etc.). Even though the instructions aren't traditional battle plans, Joshua has faith in God and follows them to the letter. He knows that only the Lord will be glorified through the victory, and Joshua does not try to add any of his own flair or ideas in order to gain his own notoriety. His obedience is pure and not mixed with any self-promotion or ambition.

The way Joshua approached decisions and promptings from God shows us that his dedication and love for God were pure. He did not have mixed motives or multiple masters. We can learn from Joshua by approaching our own decisions and promptings in a way that is solely about honoring God. In this way, we can work to keep our hearts pure and clean.

To think and pray about:

1. Joshua 4:14 says, "That day the Lord exalted Joshua in the sight of all Israel; and they stood in awe of him all the days of his life, just as they had stood in awe of Moses." This verse takes place in the relative beginning of Joshua's command: and it shows that he was very respected and powerful. This is significant because it would

have been so easy for him to become prideful and act accordingly. When we have the favor of people, we often want to keep it. And when we have talents or authority, it is difficult for us not to seek at least some glory for ourselves. Is there a type of service you do for God that is relatively easy for you to accomplish? Ask God to show you if your motives have become prideful or if you are serving with a pure heart.

2. Can you think of another Biblical character who exhibits a purity of heart? What lessons can we learn from them or from Joshua?

Dear Lord, thank you for teaching us about being pure in heart. Thank you for showing us that if our motives are mixed, or we are trying to serve multiple masters, then we are not entirely dedicated to you. Our vision of you and your will becomes cloudy when we harbor impurities. Please help us learn to let go of everything that is not you and any glory that is not yours. We love you, Lord. In Jesus' Name, Amen!

35

Pure in Heart: Stumbling Blocks

*"Blessed are the pure in heart, for they will see God." –**Matthew 5:8***

Isn't God's timing brilliantly perfect? Just this past week, I had an opportunity to understand what can keep us from being pure in heart: our will. I had been enjoying some peaceful daydreams about the future—realistic ones—when a new and unexpected opportunity for our family presented itself. An opportunity that would dramatically change the tidy image of what I had planned for the next year or two. I listened to the opportunity and remained highly skeptical. I didn't really want to hear about it, and I retained a hardened heart to the possibility.

After a few days, I began to recognize what was wrong: I had an impure heart about the situation! I was allowing my plans, my dreams, my comforts, etc., to get in the way of hearing God's thoughts on everything. My will was preventing me from seeing God's will. It's not about whether or not God wants us to pursue this new opportunity; the point is that I was unwilling to listen and made an initial assumption that it definitely couldn't be in God's plans to disrupt my own.

Following our own will before God's leads to an impure heart. It leads to obvious sins when we pursue ungodly desires. It leads to less obvious sins when we serve God in a self-interested way. And it leads to even less obvious sins when we hold too closely to our ideas and plans. Instead, we must ask God what parts of our will fit with His. Our desires and plans are not in themselves evil, but when we put them before God's desires and plans, we allow impurities in our hearts.

It is difficult to set aside my will! I know that certain dreams are precious to me or desires that strongly pull at me. They feel almost a part of me at times. But setting these things aside when they are conflicting with God's will, is essential to maintaining the purity of my heart. My desires might not be sinful, but idolizing them is.

Our heart's devotion must purely be to God's will and God's will alone. We should be happy to serve Him, and He says He will give us the desires of our hearts (Psalm 37:4). Following God's will is not a complete abandonment of our own, rather a reprioritization. We trust that God will honor our obedience and that He will take care of our needs. So we only need to serve Him and not ourselves.

When we desire God's will above our own, we are much more likely to see Him at work in everything around us. Our wills can be distracting, lead us into sinful behavior, and drive a wedge in our relationship with God. We must learn to continually surrender our will so that we can be Pure in Heart—with nothing distorting our vision of the Father.

To think and pray about:

1. Do you struggle to surrender your will as I do? What is the primary reason you try to hold onto it? Fear, ambition, comfort, etc.? Ask God to help you identify an area He would have you learn to surrender—refining and purifying you in that area.

2. Matthew 6:24 says, "No one can serve two masters. Either you will hate the one and love the other, or you will be devoted to the one and despise the other. You cannot serve both God and money." In this verse, Jesus mentions money as a potential second master. However, the concept applies to our wills as well. Think about a time when you have been faced with a conflict of what God wants versus what you want—how did you end up resolving the situation? Which one did you end up hating?

3. We read Psalm 37 earlier in this study but read it again, focusing on Pure in Heart. What verses stand out to you?

Dear Lord, thank you for the timely lessons you give us. Thank you for continually refining our character and challenging strongholds that we have built-in our hearts. Thank you for showing us the impurities we have so that we may ask for your help in removing them. Lord, please help us to be patient while you refine us. Let us be willing vessels of your will, setting aside our own. Let us learn to cast aside idols—even when they at first seem innocent. Let us learn to seek first your will and your kingdom, trusting that you will take care of the desires of our hearts. We love you, Lord. In Jesus' Name, Amen!

36

Pure in Heart: Modern Example

"Blessed are the pure in heart, for they will see God." –**Matthew 5:8**

Ruth Graham, the wife of evangelist Billy Graham, is not often referenced in lists of "faith heroes." However, when reading about her life and legacy, we see that she is someone whose faith should be remembered. Ruth's devotion to God, her husband, and her family show us that her heart was pure.

Unwavering faith, untainted by self-interest or fleshly desires, is what kept Ruth going each day. She was born in China to missionary parents. As she grew up, Ruth felt that she, too would one day be a missionary. When she met Billy Graham, she tried to convince him to go to Tibet with her to be a missionary. However, Billy had a strong conviction that he was to be an evangelist. Billy asked her, "Do you believe that God has brought us together?" She did. "In that case," he replied, "God will lead me, and you will do the following." This conversation set the stage for their future—one where they would look to God for direction and not to their desires. As one article put it: "God used her desire to go to Tibet to test her willingness to obey Him."

The Grahams had five children. While Billy traveled for so many months at a time, Ruth stayed home to raise the children in a godly way. Despite the great fame that Billy acquired, Ruth never sought to put the spotlight on herself. Instead, she focused on the ministry that she WAS called to do. Her daughter, Anne, said about Ruth, "She has the heart of an evangelist. Although her gift is often overshadowed by my father's, Mother's gift is exercised effectively on behalf of individuals. At her deepest core is the desire for individuals to know Christ in a personal and intimate way. My father preaches sermons to the masses, reaching thousands; my mother talks to individuals, loving them one by one."

Ruth was dedicated to God throughout her entire life. She was continually focused on reading the Bible and praying. When her children misbehaved or got into trouble, she didn't complain, and she just prayed even more. She seemed to become an expert at avoiding the distractions or motives that so many of us succumb to in one season or another: her heart was purely focused on God first.

Here are some tidbits of wisdom she gained through her close and consistent walk with God:

- "My job is to take care of the possible and to trust God with the impossible."
- "Worship and worry cannot live in the same heart: they are mutually exclusive."
- "Just pray for a tough hide and a tender heart."
- "Down through the years, I turned to the Bible and found in it all that I needed."
- "We cannot pray and remain the same."

Ruth's life can be an inspiration to us. It was not easy or perfect, but because she kept her heart pure and focused on God, she found the strength and wisdom needed to remain in God's will for her life.

To think and pray about:

1. Do you know anyone in your life who sets the example of being pure in heart? In what ways do you recognize this?
2. Proverbs 16:2 says, "All a person's ways seem pure to them, but motives are weighed by the Lord." How can you take steps to make sure your heart is truly pure and not just pure in your own eyes?
3. For more details about Ruth Graham's life, read this article. What lessons from Ruth's life inspire you to draw your heart closer to God?

Dear Lord, thank you for Ruth Graham and the quiet ministry you gave her. Thank you for her steady dedication to You and Your Word—keeping her heart pure. Lord, please help us to learn from her example some practical ways we can be more dedicated to you.

Show us the things in our own lives we need to address and give us more godly examples to follow. We love you, Lord. In Jesus' Name, Amen!

37

Pure in Heart: Challenge

*"Blessed are the pure in heart, for they will see God." –**Matthew 5:8***

It is a challenge for me to come up with a "Pure in Heart challenge" because it forces me to address my own struggles with maintaining a pure heart! I don't always want to address certain things! But becoming Pure in Heart requires removing anything we might be giving higher priority than our relationship with God. Obviously, anything we put ahead of Him is important to us, so surrendering it, or removing it, can be painful. The more we struggle to surrender a particular item—the more it proves to God and us that it needs to go.

Take, for instance, my oldest son's sleep habits. It has been difficult to put him to bed since birth! He will never admit to being tired, even when sick or having stayed up late the night before. As his mom, I can tell when he needs a little extra rest. When I mention to him that he needs to go to bed early, he will start arguing. He will tell me all the reasons why he isn't tired and doesn't need more sleep. But then, as his arguments do not sway me, he will get emotional. Tears might creep into the corners of his eyes as he tells me how unfair it all is. And that's where I say, "Son, your behavior right now is proving my point. If you were well-rested, you would not be this upset about such a small thing. You need to trust me and obey."

I act like my son before God sometimes! I know my convictions, but I don't want to listen to the wisdom of obeying them. Yet the more I delay in surrendering something, the more the stronghold is proven. And these things, which I value before God, are impurities in my heart.

So the challenge this week is this: identify a conviction in your life you've been avoiding or something precious to you that you've allowed to become more precious than the Will of God. Does the thought of obeying the conviction cause you to wrinkle your nose or cringe? Does the idea of giving up something precious make you want to throw a little adult tantrum? Your reaction may prove to you that you are, in fact, idolizing something before God, and therefore distorting your view of Him because of an impure heart.

Once you identify a conviction or idol, ask God to help you handle the situation in a way that honors Him. Afterward, take note, did your view of God get any clearer or change at all? Jesus said that "Blessed are the pure in heart, for they will see God." So, as we remove impurities, we should be able to see God more and more clearly in our lives. We should be able to recognize His hand that much more easily. And we should be able to see His will for our lives and the next step He has for us to take.

To think and pray about:

1. In what area of your life are you desperate to see God? Ask Him to show you what in your heart might be blocking your vision!

2. Does the thing you need to surrender, or the conviction you need to obey, come quickly to mind? I know mine do! But if you are struggling to identify heart impurities separating you from God, ask Him to reveal what He would like you to address.

3. Surrender and obedience often feel like battles we must overcome. However, leaning on bold scriptures can help us remember our authority in Christ. 2 Corinthians 10:5 says, "We demolish arguments and every pretension that sets itself up against the knowledge of God, and we take captive every thought to make it obedient to Christ."

Dear Lord, thank you for this day. Thank you for each day that we have the opportunity to learn more about you and serve you. Lord, please show us the impurities in our hearts that you would like removed. We cannot cleanse ourselves, but you have made it possible for us to be cleansed. Lord, sometimes we cling to impurities you are trying to remove. Please help us have the strength and faith to let go of them, and therefore see you with more clarity. We love you, Lord. In Jesus' Name, Amen!

38

Pure in Heart: Conclusion

*"Blessed are the pure in heart, for they will see God." –**Matthew 5:8***

Before meditating on this verse, I thought being pure in heart meant avoiding the obvious sins: lying, adultery, stealing, etc. However, it has become more evident to me that there are subtleties to each of the 10 Commandments that cause our hearts to be impure—valuing our own will before God's is a sin and impurity—loving something before God is a sin and impurity. Having a motive of self-interest is a sin and impurity.

The good news is that God has already redeemed and accounted for all of it! He is willing and able to refine us and remove impurities. However, we must also be willing.

Here is a summary of what we have reflected on during this Beatitude:

- Pure means "not mixed or adulterated with any other substance or material." However, our sinful nature automatically disqualifies us from being pure since the sin conflicts with God's holiness. Fortunately, God can work in our lives to purify us.

- In the Bible, Joshua set an example of being pure in heart that we can learn from. Through his obedience and conviction, we can see that his heart was purely dedicated to God and not himself. Self-promotion, fear, peer pressure, and popular opinion did not cloud his motives as he led the Israelites. First, he (and Caleb) stood up to the other ten spies—telling the Israelites that God would give them the land despite the strength of the Canaanites. He also followed God's instructions to defeat Jericho, even though the plans did not make sense from a human standpoint.

- One of the biggest stumbling blocks preventing us from being pure in heart is our will. The things we want to do, or something we want to have, can conflict with God's will. When we decide to pursue our will over God's, it can reveal to us the impurities of our hearts.

- Ruth Graham was a great role model for our hearts to follow. Although she isn't remembered nearly as much as her husband, the way she handled her behind-the-scenes role reveals her dedication to God's will. Her pure heart enabled God to use her and her family for great things.

- A way to test the purity of our heart in a certain area is to imagine surrendering it. If you are very reluctant or unwilling, perhaps you value it more than God and His will.

We will never be perfectly pure in heart. However, we can allow God to work in our lives and purify us. The best part of this process is that it clears the way for us to see God! Jesus said that the pure in heart will see God, and it is a blessing. The sin and impurities cloud the vision of our hearts, so when they are removed, we gain a better understanding of how He is working. We also see Him in new ways, and this blesses our hearts—causing us to become more dedicated to His will.

To think and pray about:

1. What do you think about when you hear the phrase "pure in heart"? Has your understanding of it shifted based on your personal experiences and impurities?

2. In what area of your life would you like to see God more clearly? Ask Him to help remove anything blurring your vision of Him.

Dear Lord, thank you for the Beatitudes. Thank you for the lessons you have given us to draw us closer to you and to see you more clearly. Thank you for their simplicity and yet their depth. Lord, please help us to continue understanding and applying the concept of "pure in heart." Help us to have the determination to eliminate everything from our lives that is not of you. We love you, Lord. In Jesus' Name, Amen!

Sections 39 – 44

Peacemakers

39

Peacemakers: Definition

"Blessed are the peacemakers, for they will be called children of God." – **Matthew 5:9**

To understand what a peacemaker is, we first have to understand what peace is! When I first began defining peace, I considered it to be "an absence of conflict." I was driving at the time, so I couldn't look up the actual definition. An absence of conflict, on the surface, seems like peace. Remove problems, and then you have peace, right? But then, how are we supposed ever to have peace when our lives are so full of imperfections? We can't remove them all!

It didn't sit well with me: this definition of peace that is inherently just a void. God does not offer us voids in our life—he offers us fullness and light and goodness. When I finally got a chance to look up the dictionary definition of peace, I suddenly had a greater revelation (you could even say I had more peace about the meaning ☺).Oxford dictionary defines peace as "freedom from disturbance; tranquillity." *"Freedom from"*... is much different than "absence of." "Freedom from" disturbance or conflict means that those things do not have power over us, not that they don't exist.

The Hebrew word for peace, shalom, means "harmony, wholeness, completeness, prosperity, welfare, and tranquillity." So again, peace is not defined as an absence of distressing things but about a healthy and beneficial state of being full instead of empty, being complete rather than lacking.

So it seems like peace ultimately is more about what (or who!) governs us versus removing any need for governance. Peace is being full and satisfied. Peace is about being complete and not desperately searching for something that is missing. Godly peace is about being full of God, with no room for anything that is not of God.

But then, what is a peacemaker? If Godly peace requires God, then a human certainly can't make it from thin air. But then again, we can make nothing from thin air, for we are not God. For a human to make anything, it requires us to bring things together. To make muffins, we must get the ingredients together in the mixing bowl. To make a joke, we must bring together pieces of information that sound funny together. To make peace, we must bring the presence of God into a situation.

Jesus says that peacemakers are blessed, so there must be an inherent blessing in making peace in any or all circumstances. When we are filled with God's love, joy, strength, etc., we are free from being controlled by the conflict around us. The problems do not disappear, but we are full of peace and do not despair.

To think and pray about:

1. Have you experienced the peace of God? In what circumstances? Do you notice any common theme of when you have peace versus when you do not?

2. Read Ephesians 3:14-19. Verse 19 is a blessing saying, "That you may be filled to the measure of all the fullness of God." What strategies do you have to keep yourself full of God instead of empty or full of self? If you don't know, ask God to help you understand how to be continually in His presence and full of His Spirit.

3. Have you ever been called a peacemaker? Do people associate you with having peace, being peaceful, etc.? If no, why not?

Dear Lord, thank you for this day. Thank you for the peace that you bring us just because of your very presence. Please help us to learn to acknowledge your presence in every situation. You are always there, but we do not always allow You to fill us. Please be patient with us as we sometimes try to fill ourselves with ourselves or things of this world. We love you, Lord. In Jesus' Name, Amen!

40

Peacemakers: Biblical Example

"Blessed are the peacemakers, for they will be called children of God." –
Matthew 5:9

When we think of people full of peace, it's easy to only look at external circumstances as our measurement. For example, we might assume that someone whose life is quiet and stress-free is more at peace than someone whose life is full of hardship and unpredictability. However, when we remember that true Godly peace is obtained when we allow God's presence to enter into our situation, then we see that peace doesn't have anything to do with the situation itself. Our life can look and feel chaotic, but God's presence can still be a pillar of peace in the midst of it.

Take, for instance, King David. There are many recorded stories about him in the Bible, but the Psalms he wrote gave us particular insights into the state of his heart during these trials. Many of David's stories involve fighting and war and conflict. Yet, he leaned so heavily on God that he was able to find peace and hope despite everything else surrounding him. Psalm 3 was written when David's son, Absalom, was pursuing him with murderous intentions; what a crazy concept to even comprehend! But here is what David wrote:

> *"Lord, how many are my foes!*
> *How many rise up against me!*
> *Many are saying of me,*
> *'God will not deliver him.'*
> *But you, Lord, are a shield around me,*
> *My glory, the One who lifts my head high.*
> *I call out to the Lord,*
> *And He answers me from His holy mountain.*
> *I lie down and sleep;*

I wake again because the Lord sustains me.
I will not fear though tens of thousands
Assail me on every side.
Arise, Lord!
Deliver me, my God!
Strike all my enemies on the jaw;
Break the teeth of the wicked.
From the Lord comes deliverance.
May your blessing be on your people."

King David doesn't ignore his problems; he isn't blissfully ignorant and, therefore, at peace. Instead, he tells God what is going on—inviting the Lord to intervene. He praises God—explaining how confident he is in God's promises. And David even says that despite having killers chasing after him, he is able to sleep! He has peace because he has God.

The Psalms are full of similar lessons. David begins by sharing his troubles and despair, but then through praising God and inviting Him into the situation, David recognizes the peace that God brings. We can do the same: Pour out our troubles, lean on God's Promises, Praise Him, and find Peace.

To think and pray about:

1. Is there another Bible character you associate with peace? Why?

2. Read Psalm 27. David declares great confidence in God. Do you think that there is a correlation between confidence/faith in God and peace? Does one bring about the other?

3. Are you able to sleep during stressful times of your life? Psalm 4:8 says, "In peace, I will lie down and sleep, for you alone, Lord, make me dwell in safety." If David can confidently say that while his life is in danger, it is humbling to think of the more trivial things that have caused me to lose sleep! Perhaps that is indicative that I haven't truly invited God to be present in that part of my life.

Dear Lord, thank you for this day. Thank you for being who you are—a strong and faithful God. Thank you that we can truly lie down and have peace, even when things around us are so uncertain. Thank you for giving us the life of King David, where we can learn so much from his experiences. Please, Lord, show us how we can bring your presence into all the parts of our lives—that peace may reside there as well. We love you, Lord, in Jesus' Name, Amen!

41

Peacemakers: Stumbling Blocks

"Blessed are the peacemakers, for they will be called children of God." – **Matthew 5:9**

If being a Peacemaker means bringing God into the situation by recognizing and focusing on His presence, then the opposite of that would be turning attention to something else instead of God. If we are not focused on God, His purposes, His mercy, His grace, etc., then it usually means we are focused on ourselves and how we feel about what is happening to us.

"Focus," as a noun, means the center of attention. As much as we try to multi-task, there can only be one thing at the very center of our attention—only one true focus of our hearts. When God is at the center, we remember the peace He has given to us. He gave us peace through Jesus, long before we were born or knew we needed peace. When we are not at peace, it is not because God took our peace away, but rather, we took our eyes off of Him!

In Matthew 14, Peter got out of the boat and began walking on water towards Jesus. Verse 30 says, "But when he saw the wind, he was afraid and, beginning to sink, cried out, 'Lord, save me!'" Peter was at peace with the situation when he first got out of the boat: his focus was on Jesus. I don't think Peter's problem was seeing the wind with his physical eyes and recognizing its' existence. But Peter lost his peace when the eyes of his heart were suddenly focused on his fear instead of Jesus.

Similarly, we do not need to be blinded by the problems in our lives. "Ignorance is bliss" is not the way to peace! We can see the things that threaten our peace but keep the eyes of our hearts on God. When we shift our attention and focus to ourselves, suddenly we are miserable! We can be fearful and uncertain. We can be selfish and unmotivated towards Godly purpose. We can be unforgiving and even unkind.

Those are attitudes that are not of God—He is not in the center during those moments. Yet, when we turn our attention back to Him and His goodness, peace is found, and other things fade to the periphery. We still see them, but they aren't as sharp or important. Our situation has not changed—but our perspective has. We see God and acknowledge His presence, and we, therefore, see the peace he has already given us.

I used to have a lot of nightmares and night terrors. I would be awake in the night, afraid from what I had been dreaming and completely lacking peace. As long as my focus was on myself and my feelings about the situation, I remained frightened and unable to cope. But once I got enough presence of mind to think, I would begin singing the hymn, "Turn Your Eyes Upon Jesus." It helped to refocus me and turn my attention back to God. And where God is, peace is.

To think and pray about:

1. Do you have a recurring theme of situations where you find it difficult to focus on God instead of yourself? Do you have peace during those times? If not, ask God to be the center of your attention so that you see everything else in your periphery.

2. Read Matthew 14:22-36. What else do you notice about this story and the interaction between Peter and Jesus?

3. For me, the hymn "Turn Your Eyes Upon Jesus" is my go-to perspective changer. What is yours? If you don't have one, try finding a verse or song that speaks to the eyes of your heart and inspires them to focus on God.

Dear Lord, thank you for this day. Thank you for bringing us new opportunities each day to see you. Lord, please help remind us to look for you in every situation and to acknowledge your presence. Please help us to remember to turn our eyes to You, even in the middle of our storm of self-centered emotions. Thank you for your faithfulness in seeing us even when we fail to see you. Thank you for your gift of peace. Please help us to get in the habit of claiming it! We love you, Lord. In Jesus' Name, Amen!

42

Peacemakers: Modern Example

"Blessed are the peacemakers, for they will be called children of God." – **Matthew 5:9**

There is a long list of people who have been nominated for the Nobel Peace Prize over the years. These people have done things to "make the world a better place" and bring about peaceful resolutions to certain problems. The accomplishments are great and impactful! From a worldly perspective, these things represent peace. However, as we learn more profound and deeper lessons from the Bible, we see that peace from God is vastly different from what the world tells us peace is.

We are taught that peace is the resolution of problems—an absence of conflict—a utopian dream. But peace, from this worldly viewpoint, is truly impossible as long as there is sin in this world! We can eliminate one problem, only to be met with another. Jesus even promises us, "In this world, you will have trouble." (John 16:33) As Christians, we must find our peace despite the troubles facing us. We must bring God into our situations, and He will help us navigate them with peace. We can have peace right in the middle of a crisis, not seek peace as a prize for overcoming the problem!

An example of a Godly woman who has navigated her trials with the help of God's peace is Joni Eareckson Tada. When she was 18, Joni had an accident that left her a quadriplegic. She has been in a wheelchair for 50+ years and suffers from chronic pain. However, in spite of all that she's been through (including cancer!), Joni has ministered to countless individuals through her art, writing, speaking, and the creation of her ministry for the disability community.

She doesn't do it alone. Her faith, and the peace she has found by allowing God into her circumstances, have allowed her to continue while in pain. Her paralysis remains, her chronic pain remains, her mastectomy scars remain, and her peace in God remains. Here are a couple of excerpts from her radio show so that we can learn from her example:

> *"Hi, I'm Joni Eareckson Tada and the other day while driving to work, I felt so demoralized. I mean, the day had hardly begun, and I was in such pain. But God brought the best Scripture to mind: Psalm 119:50. "This is my comfort in my affliction, that your promises renew my life." So guess what? Right then, in the back of the van, I started to recount as many of God's promises that I could recall. All the way to work I kept saying out loud, "Lord, You're my ever-present help in trouble. Lord, You promise Your grace will sustain. You promised never to leave me or forsake me." On and on. And by the time I arrived at Joni and Friends, my pain was not gone, but I sure had God's courage. I had amazing peace. So, friend, are you struggling today? Then hold on to Psalm 119, and recount the promises of God to yourself. Then just watch Him renew your life."*

And another:

> *"I'm Joni Eareckson Tada and oh, there was a time when I was anything but satisfied in Christ. After I got out of the hospital and was sent home in my wheelchair, I felt so confined and trapped. But my confinement forced me to open my Bible and take a long, hard look at the apostle Paul, who had seen the inside of more than one small room from which there was no escape. In Philippians chapter 4, Paul says that he has "learned to be content whatever the circumstance…" I tell you, I learned and I am still learning the secret of being content.*
>
> *When you believe that Jesus Christ and His strength can see you through the worst of times, contentment shows itself in that sedate, peaceful spirit. It comes from many small and great acceptances in life. One day at a time with Christ is the key to contentment. I've learned that from a wheelchair. And you can learn it from wherever you are as well."*

And one more for kicks:

> *"Hi, I'm Joni Eareckson Tada, and I am constantly at war with myself. Let me explain. I know if God is not in His rightful place in my heart, guess who I insert there? Yep, I insert me. And when that happens, my relationships are all about me; my choices, habits, and plans are all determined by me and not God. Rather than be patient with others, I become a demanding tyrant. Now can you see why I am at war with myself? I do not trust me. The old Puritans had a saying, "Sinner, do not trust yourself." And believe me, I know the sin and the pride of which I am capable. It's why I am constantly asking the Holy Spirit to help me fight to keep*

> *Jesus on the throne of my heart. When we do that, what do you know, the Prince of Peace rules the day and the peace of Christ rules in your heart. So, friend, don't trust yourself. Your pride is too big. Let Jesus rule the day."*

Wow! What great insights she has had! Do you think that she would have more peace if her life was accident and pain-free? From an earthly perspective perhaps, but an absence of conflict is empty if our heart is not filled with God. While we do not wish pain or trials on anyone, it is wonderful to see how we can have peace when we allow God to work. The rest of John 16:33, where Jesus promises us problems, says, "But take heart! I have overcome the world." When we believe that and apply it to our lives, we can be peacemakers like Joni.

To think and pray about:

1. Who do you know, or know of, that lives a life of a peacemaker? In what ways have you seen them navigate trials with Godly peace?

2. Which of the 3 Joni excerpts stood out to you the most? Did you find conviction that you need to change something in your life or confirmation that you are already on the right track?

3. Read part of Psalm 119 (you choose the section—it's a long Psalm!). Joni mentioned reciting God's promises as a way to rediscover peace in those moments where our earthly pain is most intense. Which promises can you memorize to bring forth the next time you are facing discouragement?

Dear Lord, thank you for this day. Thank you for your salvation, your peace, and your mercy. Lord, we rejoice in your promises. We praise you for your righteous laws. We have great peace, for we love your law, and nothing can make us stumble. We wait for your salvation, and we follow your commands. Give us understanding, according to your word. We love you, Lord. In Jesus' Name, Amen!

(taken from parts of Psalm 119:162-169)

43

Peacemakers: Challenge

"Blessed are the peacemakers, for they will be called children of God." – **Matthew 5:9**

When we can learn the habit of bringing God into our situations, and therefore having peace, others notice it. Being a peacemaker is a powerful testimony of God's work in our lives. It is why Jesus says that peacemakers are called "children of God"—people recognize that indescribable and inexplicable peace that can only come from a relationship with God. They may not be able to quite put their finger on what is different about you, but they sense the peaceful presence you carry.

Having peace through Jesus is a personal blessing. We can be thankful for peace while we go through all of life's situations. However, because of our love for Him and our gratitude for the peace, He has given us, we should naturally want to share it with others.

"But in your hearts revere Christ as Lord. Always be prepared to give an answer to everyone who asks you to give the reason for the hope that you have…" -**1 Peter 3:15**

This section's challenge is to prayerfully look for an opportunity to tell someone why you have peace in your heart. Praising God for what He has done in your life allows His glory to be multiplied through you. When people acknowledge the peace you have, brushing off the reason for that peace is an insult to God.

Let's say you get a great new haircut and style. When your friends comment on how amazing your hair looks, you say, "Oh, thanks." Or maybe you say, "Yeah, it took me a long time to find a good stylist." Those things are fine to say, but wouldn't it seem more fitting to acknowledge the work of the person who did your hair? Saying something like, "She did a great job," or "Let me give you the name of the salon," or "She worked a miracle with my hair," help give credit where it's due. Accepting the compliment as though you did all the work makes it all about you. You were not the stylist; you were the beneficiary of the stylist's work and talent.

Similarly, when someone comments on our peace, even when they don't use that specific word, we should testify to God's work in our life. The peace we have is not because of us; we are the beneficiaries of God's work and grace. Shrugging it off with a "thanks" might imply that we are accepting a compliment on our own accomplishment. Or saying things like, "Yeah, I've worked hard to get to a peaceful place in my life," or "Yes, I've learned the secret to having peace in all circumstances," or "Having peace really helps me get through it all" completely discredits God's work.

Many of these potential conversations are brief and passing. Here are some suggestions of things you can say in those quick moments where you want to give God the glory:

- "Amen! God is good."
- "God has taught me a lot over the years!"
- "I'm so thankful for God's peace even in these crazy times."
- "I haven't always had peace, but by God's grace, He has taught me how to have it more and more."
- "I wouldn't be this person if not for God's work in my life!"
- "Peace is such a wonderful gift from God."
- "God deserves all the glory!"

To think and pray about:

1. Have you ever been in a situation where someone complimented you, but it was really God that they saw in you? What kind of responses have you used before? Are you quick to give God glory, or are you embarrassed to bring it up? If no one has ever commented on the peace you carry, why do you think that is?

2. Ask God to set up a situation this week that allows you to glorify Him because of the peace you have in Him. Ask Him to give you the words He would have you use.

Dear Lord, thank you for the many, many, many opportunities you give us to praise you. We do not take advantage of all of them but help us to begin glorifying you more than we already do. Help give us the courage to testify to your goodness, faithfulness, and peace. Honor our testimonies—that they may ripple out away from us and cause the enemy to tremble with their impacts. Lord, thank you for giving us so many things to be thankful for. We love you, Lord. In Jesus' Name, Amen!

44

Peacemakers: Conclusion

"Blessed are the peacemakers, for they will be called children of God." –
Matthew 5:9

Here is a summary of what we have reflected on during this Beatitude:

- Peace is not a void of everything bad, but rather it is a fullness of God's presence. So for us to become a peacemaker, we must learn how to bring God into all areas of our lives.

- David, in the Bible, shows us that he had peace despite all of the problems he faced. Through his Psalms, we see that David, by recognizing God's hand in everything, found peace.

- One of the biggest stumbling blocks that prevent us from peace is an incorrect focus. When our focus is on ourselves, we are often miserable! We were created for God's glory, not our own. So when we forget to keep God in the center of our focus, we are out of alignment with His will for our life. Instead, peace is found when we get back to having a Heavenly perspective.

- Joni Eareckson Tada is a modern example of someone who has found peace during trials. Despite being a quadriplegic for over 50 years, and suffering from cancer and chronic pain, Joni has peace because she remains determined to recognize God in each situation.

- Having godly peace is such a blessing! However, we should always look for opportunities to share this peace with others. Declaring God's work in our lives brings Him glory and can give others hope!

"The peace of God, which surpasses all understanding" (Philippians 4:7), is a gift to us when we know God. However, just as God is beyond comprehension, His peace is also beyond comprehension. When we allow God into even the most difficult parts of our lives, this inexplicable peace radiates out. The world tells us that peace comes when we have no trouble. But Godly peace is evident despite our troubles. Because of this, the world does not understand it even though they see it.

Radiating peace gets peoples' attention. Bringing peace into turmoil is noticeable. Being hopeful in peace makes us stand out. But ultimately, whether or not people realize it, when they see our peace, they see God. Jesus says that peacemakers are blessed because people will recognize them as children of God. When we carry God's presence in our hearts, we begin to resemble Him, and people take notice.

We should be very grateful for God's peace in our hearts because it helps us with our journey. But this peace is even more amazing because it reveals our Heavenly Father and acts as a testimony on His behalf: we are recognized as children of God!

To think and pray about:

1. What have you learned about being a peacemaker? Do you think Jesus would include you in His list of "blessed are the peacemakers"? Why or why not?

2. Ask God to show you how your peace (or lack thereof!) impacts the people around you. Ask Him to reveal ways that you can be a light and encouragement because of your peace in Him.

Dear Lord, thank you for your inexplicable peace. Thank you for dwelling in our hearts that we may become more like you as we get to know you better. Thank you for allowing us the opportunity to be a light to those around us, and point them to you when they see you in us. Please help us to become better peacemakers so we can glorify you even more. We love you, Lord. In Jesus' Name, Amen!

Sections 45 – 50

Persecuted Because of Righteousness

45

Persecuted: Definition

*"Blessed are those who are persecuted because of righteousness, for theirs is the kingdom of heaven." –***Matthew 5:10**

The first thing I think of whenever I hear this verse is a martyr. That is the picture of persecution: someone being killed because of their beliefs. However, in reality, that is just the extreme version of persecution. Persecute, which the word "persecution" derives from, means "to harass or punish in a manner designed to injure, grieve, or afflict. Specifically, to cause to suffer because of belief."

Jesus clarifies His statement so that it only applies to people who are persecuted because of righteousness. So, someone who is persecuted for their political beliefs, race, or opinions is not included here.

Earlier in this study, we defined righteousness as "the quality of being morally right." Therefore, Biblical righteousness is based on the rightness of God. Through this Beatitude verse, Jesus is saying that we are blessed when we are persecuted for trying to live according to God's standard.

This Beatitude stands out from the others in two significant ways. First, it is the only one where Jesus comments not on our actions but the actions of others towards us. "Poor in Spirit," "Mourn," "Meek," Hunger and Thirst," "Merciful," "Pure in Heart," and "Peacemakers" all describe our approach to our Christian walk. "Persecuted" describes the world's response to our Christian walk. How interesting that Jesus would close out His list with that!

The second major differentiator in this Beatitude is the fact that Jesus dedicates two additional sentences to it! The two following verses are:

"Blessed are you when people insult you, persecute you and falsely say all kinds of evil against you because of me. Rejoice and be glad, because great is your reward in

heaven, for, in the same way, they persecuted the prophets who were before you." –
Matthew 5:11-12

Now, to be persecuted, people have to recognize in you the thing they want to persecute. If you completely blend in with those around you, who do not share your beliefs, then why should they make you suffer for those beliefs? Your faith must be evident in order to offend the world's conflicting values. Perhaps this is why Jesus saved this Beatitude for last. If we truly put into practice the other 7 Beatitudes, then it's only a matter of time before the world notices and reacts.

To think and pray about:

1. What do you think of when you think about persecution?

2. Have you ever been persecuted because of righteousness? What was the situation? Did it reaffirm your faith or cause you to shrink away from it?

3. Why do you think Jesus included this very different Beatitude in the list?

Dear Lord, thank you for this list of verses you gave to us to learn from. Please help us to understand more and more your intentions behind the list. Thank you for the reminder that persecution is a natural consequence of obedience and that we should take comfort in knowing we are blessed when we are obedient. Please give us the faith and perseverance to not shrink away when we suffer for our faith. We love you, Lord. In Jesus' Name, Amen!

46

Persecuted: Biblical Example

*"Blessed are those who are persecuted because of righteousness, for theirs is the kingdom of heaven." –***Matthew 5:10**

In the Bible, there are many, many stories of persecution. It seems like stories of persecution are more prevalent than stories of all the other Beatitudes combined! Here are some of the more noteworthy ones:

- Daniel was persecuted for praying to only God and not King Darius. (Daniel 6)

- Joseph was persecuted by Potiphar's wife because she did not like that he stood by his convictions. (Genesis 39)

- Job was persecuted by the Devil because of his righteousness (Job 1)

- Elijah was persecuted by Jezebel for standing up to the prophets of Baal. (1 Kings 19)

- Nehemiah was persecuted for rebuilding the walls of Jerusalem (Throughout the book of Nehemiah)

- Stephen was persecuted (and killed!) for teaching about Jesus. (Acts 6)

None of these men likely felt blessed while being persecuted! Being ridiculed, black-listed, beaten, imprisoned, or killed are not the outcomes we strive for when we obey God. So why does Jesus say that we are blessed when we are persecuted because of righteousness? From an earthly perspective, it would seem that persecution is a curse. An indication that we are doing the wrong thing. An indication that God is displeased with our efforts. An indication that maybe we worship a powerless God.

However, when we look more deeply at stories of persecution, we see that while persecution may feel like a pit—it is actually a platform. Persecution because of our obedience to God sets the stage for Him to be glorified in an amplified manner. If we look at the previous stories again, from a Heavenly perspective, we can see how God used them to advance His plans and glorify Himself.

- Daniel was persecuted for praying to only God and not King Darius. (Daniel 6) But then God miraculously saved Daniel from the lions' den, therefore proving His power to the unbelievers.

- Joseph was persecuted by Potiphar's wife because she did not like that he stood by his convictions. (Genesis 39) Joseph was then thrown into prison, where he made connections that would eventually save his family from famine.

- Job was persecuted by the Devil because of his righteousness. (Job 1) Then God restored what had been taken from Job. This created a timeless narrative that proved that any damage the enemy can do, God can restore to something even greater than what was previously there.

- Elijah was persecuted by Jezebel for standing up to the prophets of Baal. (1 Kings 19) This persecution caused Elijah to flee and set the stage for him to hear God's gentle whisper. It also triggered the need for the calling of Elisha—the next great prophet.

- Nehemiah was persecuted for rebuilding the walls of Jerusalem. (Throughout the book of Nehemiah) Each time he was ridiculed or threatened, Nehemiah responded with faith and prayer. These trials strengthened him as a leader, and he was able to remain focused on his conviction to complete the wall while encouraging the workers.

- Stephen was persecuted (and killed!) for teaching about Jesus. (Acts 6) After Stephen was stoned to death, the gospel began to spread further because the persecution caused the church to scatter.

Each story of persecution reveals a glimpse of God's intricate tapestry He is weaving throughout history. So, although being persecuted for righteousness is not pleasant, we can take comfort in these stories of how God has used persecution to highlight His victory over darkness.

To think and pray about:

1. What other Bible stories come to mind when you think of persecution? How do you see God's glory in them?

2. Read Acts 5:17-42. The passage is about the persecution of the Apostles. What stands out to you in the story?

3. Acts 5:41 says that "The apostles left the Sanhedrin, rejoicing because they had been counted worthy of suffering disgrace for the Name." Have you ever been pleased when faced with opposition to your faith? Why or why not?

Dear Lord, thank you for all of the stories of the Bible. Thank you for the repetition and patterns that teach us valuable lessons. You show us the same things, over and over, in new ways so that we can learn more and more deeply. Please continue to teach us the value of persecution. Help us to see it from a Heavenly perspective and as a blessing, even when it feels painful. Please continue to use us to advance your Kingdom. We love you, Lord. In Jesus' Name, Amen!

47

Persecuted: Stumbling Blocks

*"Blessed are those who are persecuted because of righteousness, for theirs is the kingdom of heaven." —**Matthew 5:10***

Unlike the other Beatitudes, this one is less of a goal and more of a consequence. Our goal is not to be persecuted, but Jesus acknowledges that being righteous often leads to persecution. One of the biggest stumbling blocks preventing us from experiencing this Beatitude is fear.

It is much easier to do the right thing when we are surrounded by support and encouragement. It is also relatively easy to obey when we know that the results of that obedience will feel good. On the other hand, being righteous when we fear the response of others is much more difficult. It is difficult when we fear the results of our obedience. Obedience in the face of adversity, real or imagined, can be frightening!

Fortunately, the Bible is full of reminders that encourage us towards righteousness instead of fear. When our resolve is wavering, we can cling to verses like these to remind us that righteousness is more valuable than anything we lose due to persecution:

- **Romans 12:21** "Do not overcome evil by evil, but overcome evil with good."
- **John 14:21** "Whoever has my commands and keeps them is the one who loves me. The one who loves me will be loved by my Father, and I too will love them and show myself to them."
- **Galatians 6:9** "Let us not become weary in doing good, for at the proper time we will reap a harvest if we do not give up."

- **Deuteronomy 3:22** (Moses to Joshua) "Do not be afraid of them; the Lord, your God himself, will fight for you."

- **Isaiah 41:10** "So do not fear, for I am with you; do not be dismayed, for I am your God. I will strengthen you and help you; I will uphold you with my righteous right hand. All who rage against you will surely be ashamed and disgraced; those who oppose you will be as nothing and perish."

We are rewarded when our desire to do right overcomes our fear of the consequence. With each step of obedience, there is a Heavenly reward, even if the earthly result is not pleasant. We must keep striving towards righteousness, no matter the earthly cost—trusting that God's ways are better than ours.

To think and pray about:

1. Read Psalm 27. David wrote this while he was being persecuted; however, take note of his confidence in the Lord! Do you have faith like this?

2. Has fear ever prevented you from obedience? What could you do in future situations to make sure that you value obedience over the potential consequence?

Dear Lord, thank you for Your Word, which can get us through any circumstance. Thank you also for the reminders that there is a Heavenly reward for obedience, even when the earthly experience is full of trials. Lord, please help us not to fear the consequences of righteousness instead of developing a love for obedience. We love you, Lord. In Jesus' Name, Amen!

48

Persecuted: Modern Example

*"Blessed are those who are persecuted because of righteousness, for theirs is the kingdom of heaven." –**Matthew 5:10***

Many people experience moments of persecution or suffering for their faith. However, there are some whose life is defined and shaped by that persecution. Watchman Nee was one of those people. One biography about his life even calls him a "man of suffering" in its title.

Watchman Nee was born in China in 1903 to Christian parents. While in high school, he became a Christian himself and decided to devote his entire life to the gospel. He chose the name "Watchman" because he wanted to be "a watchman raised up to sound out a warning call in the dark night."

Watchman Nee's ministry was far-reaching, and he also wrote many books based on his insights into the Scriptures. However, his life was also filled with suffering, as described by a biographer:

"Watchman Nee endured much suffering for the sake of the New Testament ministry. Due to his absoluteness in following the Lord and his faithfulness in fulfilling the Lord's commission, he underwent frequent mistreatment as well as lifelong hardships. As he fought the battle for the Lord's move, he was under constant attack from God's enemy, Satan. At the same time, he was also under God's sovereign hand. He recognized the sovereign arrangements of God in his environment not merely as a divinely apportioned "thorn in the flesh" but, more importantly, as a means by which God was able to deal with him. Due to both Satan's attacks and God's faithful environmental dealings, Watchman Nee lived a life of suffering. The majority of his sufferings came from five sources: poverty, ill health, denominational opposition, dissenting brothers and sisters in the local churches, and imprisonment."

Watchman Nee ended up dying in prison, serving a sentence as punishment for preaching the gospel. Although his life was cut short, his insights still inspire believers today. The persecution and suffering that he experienced deepened his testimony in a way that comfort could never do. Watchman Nee understood that he must completely rely on God's strength and not his own. In his book, "The Normal Christian Life," he wrote:

> *"Living in the Spirit means that I trust the Holy Spirit to do in me what I cannot do myself. This life is completely different from the life I would naturally live of myself. Each time I am faced with a new demand from the Lord, I look to him to do in me what he requires of me. It is not a case of trying but of trusting; not of struggling but of resting in him. If I have a hasty temper, impure thoughts, a quick tongue or a critical spirit, I shall not set out with a determined effort to change myself, but instead, reckoning myself dead in Christ to these things, I shall look to the Spirit of God to produce in me the needed purity of humility or meekness, confident that he will do so. This is what it means to "stand still, and see the salvation of the Lord, which he will work for you" (Exodus 14:13)."*

God used the suffering of Watchman Nee—it was not wasted. Let us also learn to do what is right in the face of adversity—trusting that God is in charge of redeeming and using any consequences of our righteousness.

To think and pray about:

1. What other stories of modern persecution do you know? Do they scare your faith or inspire it?
2. Read Exodus 14:13-14. Are you in the habit of letting God fight your battles? What is a battle that you have been trying to win on your own? How can you apply the wisdom of Watchman Nee to that situation?

Dear Lord, thank you for the ministry and wisdom of Watchman Nee. Thank you for his determination to follow You, at any physical cost to himself. Lord, please show us how to apply his example to our hearts. Show us how we can be still and let You develop us and let You fight for us. We love you, Lord. In Jesus' Name, Amen!

49

Persecuted: Challenge

"Blessed are those who are persecuted because of righteousness, for theirs is the kingdom of heaven." –**Matthew 5:10**

Being persecuted in any form is not fun. It doesn't feel good to be insulted or assaulted because of our pursuit of righteousness. And yet, even fellow Christians sometimes put each other down because they do not understand individual callings or convictions.

I think sometimes it is more challenging to face the disapproval of a friend than the overt persecution of a non-believer. However, our desire for comfortable unity should never compromise what we sincerely believe God calls us to do. Paul knew that even Christians would not always be convicted of the same things, and he addressed this in Romans 14 and into chapter 15.

"We who are strong ought to bear with the failings of the weak and not to please ourselves. Each of us should please our neighbors for their good, to build them up. For even Christ did not please himself but, as it is written: "The insults of those who insult you have fallen on me." For everything that was written in the past was written to teach us, so that through the endurance taught in the Scriptures and the encouragement they provide we might have hope." –**Romans 15:1-4**

The challenge for this week is twofold:

The first part is to reflect upon an existing situation or prepare your heart for an upcoming one, where you are tempted to criticize another Christian's convictions. If what they are doing does not obviously go against the Word of God, is it helpful to criticize and judge? Pray about any response or feedback before you give it to them—making sure you are acting for their good and not just to make yourself feel good.

Secondly, is there a conviction on your heart that you have been hesitating to act upon? Like Romans 15:4 says, find encouragement and endurance in the scriptures. Follow through with your convictions, even if persecution seems like the consequence.

I am not discouraging healthy debate or seeking wisdom from others. This challenge refers to when we don't want to act in faith because we fear the opinions of those around us. Persecution takes many forms, including passive-aggressiveness, insults, withholding what someone needs, physical assault, and judgement. Let us take care to continue towards righteousness despite these things being used against us, and also avoid persecuting others unintentionally.

To think and pray about:

1. Pray about how to move forward in the conviction that you have been pushing aside. Ask God to give you wisdom on how to peaceably proceed, but also the strength to seek His approval above the approval of others.

2. Pray for God to soften your heart towards the convictions of others, even when you do not understand them.

3. 2 Timothy 3:12 says, "In fact, everyone who wants to live a godly life in Christ Jesus will be persecuted." Does this promise make you want to live a godly life? How can you prepare yourself to handle any kind of persecution that is coming to you?

Dear Lord, thank you for the teachings of Paul. He knew both sides of persecution: persecuting others and being persecuted. Please help us learn how to apply his wisdom to our own experiences. Give us insight into what we should do and show us where we need to extend grace to others. We love you, Lord. In Jesus' Name, Amen!

50

Persecuted: Conclusion

"Blessed are those who are persecuted because of righteousness, for theirs is the kingdom of heaven." –**Matthew 5:10**

Persecution is not a blessing. It is not even something to strive for, making it a unique item in the Beatitudes list. Yet Jesus included it and ended with it, which gives it great significance.

Here is a summary of what we have reflected on during this Beatitude:

- "Persecute" means "to cause to suffer because of belief." For us to be persecuted for being a Christian seeking after righteousness, the world must be able to recognize that we are not the same as it.

- The Bible has many, many stories about persecution. When we look at these stories closely, we see that persecution is a platform God can use to advance His plans and glorify Himself.

- One of the biggest reasons we may not be recognized as Christ-followers, and therefore avoid any persecution is fear. But when our desire to be obedient to God outweighs our fear of the consequence, we will be blessed.

- Watchman Nee had a ministry in China and suffered greatly for it. However, his dedication to God is still inspiring people today!

- Persecution comes in many forms and sometimes is even inflicted by fellow Christians. It is important for us to focus on our own convictions and extend grace to others.

Persecution is evidence of the fruit we are bearing through the other Beatitudes. When being poor in spirit, mourning, meekness, hungering, and thirsting for righteousness, mercy, purity of heart, and peacemaking become part of our identities—it is only a matter of time before people notice that we are not of this world.

Jesus says that those who are persecuted because of righteousness have the Kingdom of Heaven. This is the same promise He used at the beginning of the list—paired with "poor in spirit,"; bringing everything full-circle. This is a relevant connection because experiencing persecution leads us to be poor in spirit. When we suffer, we quickly remember how much we need God. Also, when we remember this Beatitude, with the promise of the Kingdom of Heaven, our perspective on our situation shifts upward. We can be encouraged in the midst of our suffering—knowing that it is because we are actually on a righteous track.

To think and pray about:

1. Read John 15:18-25. Why do you think that Jesus said that the world hates Him? Why do you think that the world hates the people that follow Jesus?

2. What has stood out, or convicted you, the most about this Beatitude? Have you come away with any new perspective on persecution and suffering?

Dear Lord, thank you for this Beatitude. Thank you for connecting it to the others and bringing the list full circle. Thank you also for Your reminders about Your persecution. Please help us to continue to look up to you when we face trouble for our obedience. We love you, Lord. In Jesus' Name, Amen!

Sections 51 – 52

Conclusion

51

Conclusion: Full Circle

"Blessed are the poor in spirit, for theirs is the Kingdom of Heaven.
Blessed are those who mourn, for they will be comforted.
Blessed are the meek, for they will inherit the earth.
Blessed are those who hunger and thirst for righteousness, for they will be filled.
Blessed are the merciful, for they will be shown mercy.
Blessed are the pure in heart, for they will see God.
Blessed are the peacemakers, for they will be called children of God.
Blessed are those who are persecuted because of righteousness, for theirs is the Kingdom of Heaven."
–Matthew 5:3-10

At first glance, the Beatitudes seem like just a "to do" list. However, spending time meditating on them reveals how alive and connected they all are. Jesus begins by encouraging us to be **Poor in Spirit**; essentially, we need to acknowledge that we are nothing without God. Then, when we feel our complete dependence on God, we also begin to see how much the world also needs God. Seeing the brokenness of the world causes us to **Mourn** the need for, but appreciate the promise of, salvation.

Our gratitude for that salvation motivates us to be **Meekly** obedient to God's instructions. The more we obey and experience the joy that comes from obedience, we **Hunger and Thirst** for more of that righteousness. Once we are in the habit of seeking God's righteousness, we are therefore in the habit of surrendering our *right* to anything. Instead, we can more quickly extend **Mercy** because we understand that everything we are, and everything we have, belongs to God and not us.

This renewed perspective of who we are compared to who God is, challenges us to have no idols before Him, resulting in **Purity of Heart**. When our heart is therefore looking constantly to God, with nothing hindering the view, we naturally bring Him into all aspects of our lives. This leads us to be recognized by others as children of God because we have therefore become **Peacemakers**. Once we have been identified as God's children, we are vulnerable to being **Persecuted**. This persecution brings the whole list full-circle because it renews our dependence on God, reminding us to remain **Poor in Spirit**.

Does anything else even need to be said? The wisdom of Jesus' "to do" list is astounding! Instead of being individual disciplines that we must attempt to learn on our own, this is a list of a chain reaction that occurs when we humble ourselves before God. It all begins with recognizing that we need God and that heart posture takes us on a journey of additional lessons and blessings.

To think and pray about:

1. Experiencing the chain-reaction of the Beatitudes is not a one-time thing but rather a circular journey that takes us deeper and deeper each time we go around. In what way have you recognized a connection between the Beatitudes in your own life?

2. Which is the most challenging Beatitude for you to embrace? Do you think that your lack of progress in that area is holding you back in others?

3. Read Matthew 11:28-30. In verse 29, Jesus tells us that He is humble in heart and that we should learn from Him. If humility is the key to "unlocking" the cycle of the Beatitudes, then studying more about how Jesus lived will unlock additional insights into how we should be living our lives and experiencing God's best.

Dear Lord, thank you for the wisdom of the Beatitudes. Thank you for showing us how they are not just empty words and promises but rather a living and breathing list of characteristics lived out by Jesus. As we strive to be more like Him in an effort to glorify You, please help us. Give us further and further wisdom and strength as we daily choose to recognize our need for You. We love you, Lord. In Jesus' Name, Amen!

52

Conclusion: Walking with the Beatitudes

"Blessed are the poor in spirit, for theirs is the Kingdom of Heaven.
Blessed are those who mourn, for they will be comforted.
Blessed are the meek, for they will inherit the earth.
Blessed are those who hunger and thirst for righteousness, for they will be filled.
Blessed are the merciful, for they will be shown mercy.
Blessed are the pure in heart, for they will see God.
Blessed are the peacemakers, for they will be called children of God.
Blessed are those who are persecuted because of righteousness, for theirs is the Kingdom of Heaven." **–Matthew 5:3-10**

After an intentional study, the Beatitudes are alive! It's amazing how our understanding can grow when we take the time to listen to the Holy Spirit. How has your view of the Beatitudes evolved over this study? Take some time to read through the Beatitudes again, and then summarize them in a way that reminds you of their depth. Here is how I would write the Beatitudes in an effort to make them applicable to my daily life:

- **Poor in Spirit**: Blessed are those who depend on God and fully trust Him, for they have access to everything in His Kingdom.

- **Mourn:** Blessed are those who, alongside the Holy Spirit, grieve the consequences of sin—for they have a deeply rooted hope in the power of redemption.

- **Meek:** Blessed are those who continually submit to God's authority because they will be trusted with stewarding His creation.

- **Hunger & Thirst:** Blessed are those who seek to do God's will because it is right, not for the results, for they will be satisfied by their obedience.

- **Merciful:** Blessed are those who give up their rightful claim to justice, for they will have a greater understanding of the mercy God has shown us.

- **Pure in Heart:** Blessed are those who value their relationship with God before all else, for they will have an unclouded view of how He is working in their life.

- **Peacemakers:** Blessed are those who allow God to permeate their every situation, for others will recognize that they are set apart from this world.

- **Persecuted:** Blessed are those who face consequences on earth for doing right, for they will receive a Heavenly reward.

Will you keep walking with the Beatitudes in your heart?

Dear Lord, thank you for sending Jesus. Thank you for all of the parables and teachings that He gave us. Please help us to develop an even greater desire to learn Your ways and follow You. Lord, please show us how to keep the wisdom of the Beatitudes in our hearts. We love you, Lord. In Jesus' Name, Amen!

ABOUT KHARIS PUBLISHING

KHARIS PUBLISHING is an independent, traditional publishing house with a core mission to publish impactful books, and channel proceeds into establishing mini-libraries or resource centers for orphanages in developing countries, so these kids will learn to read, dream, and grow. Every time you purchase a book from Kharis Publishing or partner as an author, you are helping give these kids an amazing opportunity to read, dream, and grow. Kharis Publishing is an imprint of Kharis Media LLC. Learn more at https://www.kharispublishing.com.

www.ingramcontent.com/pod-product-compliance
Lightning Source LLC
Chambersburg PA
CBHW070157100426
42743CB00013B/2946